MILLIONAIRE'S
MIND

9 Steps to Your
Million dollar Business

Rudy Mutombo

To order additional copies of this book, contact the Publisher:
Rudy Mutombo Business Coaching LLC,
1825 Walnut Hill Ln., Ste. 120
Irving, Texas 75038
Phone Number: 866-231-8251
Fax: 214-614-8436
Email Address: info@rudymutombo.com
Website: www.rudymutombo.com

Contents

Acknowledgement

I would like to give a special thanks to God for giving me the grace and insight for this book. I would also like to use this moment to acknowledge my spiritual mentors, Apostle Guy Joseph Tanoh and Prophet Zogo, for their guidance.

A special recognition goes to my father, Johnny Mutangilay, who has always been my number one source of inspiration and motivation. A big thank you also goes to the wonderful team behind me, led by my indefatigable Brand Manager, Raissa Musau. Your efforts are well appreciated and you are the real stars of the show.

I would also like to acknowledge the efforts of Richard Iroko and Shamarr Mason for bringing this project to fruition. Thanks to Aurelia Joao and Jude Bampende for always believing in me and for supporting my vision.

Lastly, I want to thank all my clients and customers who have patronized my businesses. May God continue to enlarge your territories.

Foreword

Not many business owners would boldly expose their faith. Most would rather serve God in secret. Well, that is not the case for Rudy Mutombo. He is a man of exceptional talent, and his ability to keep multiple businesses running is worth looking into. I have known Rudy for many years now, and I can honestly say that he's one of the most outstanding and compassionate entrepreneurs you will ever meet. Rudy Mutombo is a brilliant young man who stands out. Anything he touches becomes extremely fruitful. Him writing a book about business for business owners is surely a God thing. As you read this book, I believe divine deposits of wisdom and understanding will be released into your life. Rudy Mutombo's *Millionaire's Mind* series of books will surely prepare you for good success.

—Apostle Guy Joseph Tanoh

Introduction

Being a Christian is not an excuse to be poor. Does God want you to be wealthy? Well, the Bible is filled with an abundance of financial guidance that could trigger your prosperity. There are keys to prosperity in the Bible and it is only a matter of applying the right keys to unlock your million-dollar business. The aim of this book is to guide you through the Biblical principles that apply to business, as you take the steps towards your million-dollar business.

"Dishonest money dwindles away, but he who gathers money little by little makes it grow." Proverbs 13: 11 (NIV)

When I first delved into entrepreneurship, I just wanted to make money for *myself.* As the years went on, I took the focus off me, and decided to start training *others* how to make money. No matter what your business idea is, the business principles discussed in this book can be applied to your business, and will allow your business to experience outstanding success. In this book, I will discuss a step by step business model that will give you a clear vision for your million-dollar business. The same business models are used by successful multinational company owners. I will also provide Bible verses for support since the Bible is filled with successful businessmen, as well as many business principles. Consider this book as your eye opener to the unlimited potentials you have as a business owner and as a Christian.

This book will cover many important factors, such as understanding your 'why' and determining 'what' business you want to establish, as well as determining the target market. This book is an ultimate guide equipped with the information and tools you need to start that million-dollar business. How can you attract customers and keep them as customers long-term? Sam Walton famously said, "There is only one boss. The customer. And he can fire everybody in the company from the chairman on down, simply by spending his money somewhere else". The knowledge this book provides will equip you beyond measures.

Set your dreams alight by taking the nine effective strides to your million-dollar business.

CHAPTER ONE

Understanding Your Why

U nderstanding your 'why' is crucial to setting up a business as the business itself. Your, 'why' is the purpose of your business, and a defined purpose is a recipe for success. In the beginning of creation, in Genesis 1:26, God said: *"Let us make man in our own image."* He was clearly defining the purpose of creation. According to William Barclay, "There are two great days in a person's life–the day we are born and the day we discover why." A goal becomes a reality through focus, determination, and smart work. The first step to setting up a million-dollar business is *Understanding Your Why*. What does this mean? Michael Hyatt famously quoted, "When you know your WHY, you know your way." This statement is also true in business. Your 'why' is your purpose, and aligning it with execution is key to setting up a successful business. Your 'why' is your Mission Statement and that is what sets you apart from other businesses.

MISSION STATEMENT

A mission statement defines the existence of an organization. When I became an entrepreneur, my mission statement was to make money by all means, for myself, Rudy Mutombo. It took me a few years to understand that the mission statement has to be bigger than myself; it has to be bigger than *me*. Then, my focus changed and evolved to making my customers successful by all means. Your mission statement should identify who your primary targets or audience are, the products and services you offer, as well as your geographical proximity. The mission statement is simply the purpose of the business, but it is a vital component of setting up a business entity. It does not necessarily have to be witty, but having a mission statement that is accurate and informative is an important key point. It is as important as the business plan itself—a mission statement captures the essence of the business goals.

Your mission statement indicates what your business is all about to your customers, employees, suppliers, and the community at large. Your mission statement should reflect every facet of your business, such as the essence and scope of the products and services you offer, pricing, quality, and growth potential. A mission statement also provides clear directions about the business and keeps the team on track. Like Andy Stanley famously said, "Direction, not your intention that determines your destination." A defined mission statement also helps to align a business from the owner, new hires, to the entire team, and ensures everyone is on the same page in terms of business goals. When your team understands what you do and why you do it, it leads to more efficiency.

Mission statements demonstrate your business values to both employees and customers; it is not just a statement of desire to be the best in the field or make the best products. Instead, it is a way of showing what makes your company stand out.

This is your, 'Why'. Understanding this would also help shape the future of your business as it becomes a navigational tool over time. By identifying the, 'Why', the mission statement of your business, you will be equipped to understand the goals your company is committed to accomplish. It also serves as a strong foundation for you to build and expand your business. Even the Bible emphasizes the importance of a strong foundation. It is the bedrock of your business. "Matthew 7: 24 says: *Everyone then who hears these words of mine and does them will be like a wise man who built his house on the rock. And the rain fell, and the floods came and the winds blew and beat on that house but it did not fall, because it had been founded on the rock.*"

The biggest business corporations have consistently excelled at aligning the 'Why' with execution; thereby, enjoying sales and profits. Customers do not buy 'what' you do or 'how' you do it, but 'why' you do it. Mission statements do not only shape how a business should act, but it also shapes how individual employees approach their job, and this builds the business culture. It removes uncertainty in an employee's mind. Understanding core business values of the organization would propel employees to be more effective. Apart from setting the standard internally amongst the work force, it is the strongest statement you can send to the public. Customers and clients would find the mission statement an encapsulation of your business values. The statement conveys the passion and vision of the business in a way that would intrigue and reassure the general public. Establishing and understanding your 'why' leads to the next stage: Product or Service?

PRODUCT OR SERVICE

As a business owner, develop the trait or ability to select and offer the right products and services to consumers in a highly competitive market. Your ability to make sound choices determines the success or failure of your business venture. Products and services change with time and tide; some of the products and services offered eight years ago are different from what's being offered today. These same products and services offered today will also not necessarily be in demand five to eight years from now–so the cycle continues. A smart business owner has to make sound decisions. There is a plethora of products and services available to consumers with unlimited opportunities to enter the marketplace with a new product or service and compete favorably. Your skill at choosing the right product or the right service to offer determines how you are able to compete with what's being offered. A lot of thinking goes into deciding what product or service to offer. Once you have identified a product or service, you must be personally committed to make it successful. What kinds of products do you like or enjoy? Can you see yourself getting excited about this particular product or service? Do you *like* the product or service you are about to sell? Would you buy and use it yourself?

Your Product or Service section of the business plan is what sets you apart from competitors in the market place. Your Product or Service section should aim to clearly define what product and/or services you are selling with emphasis on the value you are providing to your customers and clients. This part of your business plan should have a detailed look at all elements related to the products or services you have to offer. The following tips are essential:

- Products or Service Description
- Comparison to Similar Products or Service
- List of Price Points
- Explanation (How Product or Service orders would be fulfilled)
- Overview of any special software, supplies, or technology required for your Product or Service
- Outline of Future Product or Services

The purpose of the Product or Service section of a business is to clearly express the benefits you are providing to your customers or clients as a business owner. All information supplied should be focused on this goal while thinking, "Why should my ideal consumer patronize my product or service?" Outline the need your product or service is meeting, the problems it solves, and the overall purpose of the product or service. Keep it simple while also clearly highlighting the basic information, as well as your unique selling point. The bulk of the Product or Service Section should focus on the end result, but information about pricing is equally vital as well, such as the details of how a product or service will be sold, where it will be retailed online and etc. This leads us into the next phase: What Core Values are you delivering to your customers with your Product or Service?

CORE VALUES

Core values are the fundamental beliefs of a business owner or business organization. These are the guiding principles that dictate behavior in the business and can help people understand the difference between right and wrong. Identifying the core values of your business will help you to find clarity, tackle ambiguity, and make good decisions. Your core values also help determine if you are fulfilling your business goals. Why are core values important in business? They support the vision, as well as shape what the company values are. In essence, your core values are your identity as a business. Establishing strong core values provides internal and external advantages to your business. It helps in decision-making processes; for instance, if your core value is quality, any product not reaching the quality standard is automatically eliminated.

Core Values inform clients and customers what your business is about and clarifies the identity of your business. You can hold the same core values as your competitors as long as it is authentic to your company and employees. In a highly competitive world, identifying and devoting specific values to your customers gives you a comparative advantage. These values that you provide to your customers differentiate you from the competition and help you carve a *niche*. Think about how many brands you patronize and how easily you can identify why you patronize them. Core values are timeless and do not change. Over time, they become the actual identity of the business. People will remember the value your business brings, and then patronize you for that value, hence, the need for strong core values.

In establishing your business's core values for your customers, it is pertinent to ask yourself the following questions:

Would I hold on to these values tomorrow if I have enough money to retire?
Would these values be valid 100 years from now?
Would I want my business to maintain these values even if at some point, they become comparative disadvantages?

These questions are important because it helps to draw a line between core values and strategy. Strategies and business plans change over time but core values are fixed regardless of time or factors. In many cases, the customer is the key to your business prospects, not the competition. Every product and service give customers the benefits on whether they are willing to pay the price attached to it. This is the value that the customer attaches to the product or service. Knowing fully well the customer has other options, it is the value provided by a particular product or service that earns money.

The strength of purchase by any consumer is the strength of value of the customer ascribes to the product. The value of a product or service is the most amount of money customers are willing to pay. This means that, a customer will not purchase a product or service whose price exceeds the value. Aim to learn from past examples of customer satisfaction: What gave a consumer the most satisfaction? This serves as a compass to evaluate your standards. Adjusting to this means adjusting to your business's reality. The compliments you receive from a customer will come only after satisfaction of the product or service itself. Itemizing the core values you deliver to your customers not only keeps customer relations, but it serves as a moral guide for the business relationship between you, as a business owner, and a consumer/ client. This would also help you identify the solutions to the problem your product or service is offering.

SOLUTIONS TO WHAT PROBLEM
YOUR BUSINESS IS OFFERING

As an entrepreneur or an emerging business owner, do you just want to start a business or do you want to solve a problem? People will always seek new solutions and customers will also always seek better products and services. The consumer population will always look for better, faster, and smarter ways to accomplish everyday tasks. Your job, as a business owner, is to identify these problems for the consumers and how to solve them with your product or service. The biggest problem for most business owners is finding these problems and providing a matching solution. When you identify the solutions to the problem your business is offering, it helps you channel the solutions to the problem better. For example, Google made search engines better, Amazon simplified online buying and selling, while Netflix is solving on-demand streaming media. These various companies pin-pointed the problem and set about the task of achieving solutions.

To set up a million-dollar business, you need to be able to identify the problem, and then work on how your product or service would solve it for the consumer. When your product or service solves your consumer's problems, it becomes a must-have for the consumer. The consumer builds a trust with your business because it identifies a crucial problem and effectively solves the problem in question. Products with a real need are easy to market. You would not have to convince people of the problem or the need for your product or service because it is simply visible. If your product or service is not a must-have, you can re-purpose it to solve pressing needs, and then watch it turn into a must-have. You do not want to start a business that may not survive, so start by doing your homework on the problem. This will lead you to who you are going to solve it for. Validate your idea and make sure there is a real market for your business. That way, you ensure you are not setting up *just another* business. When your business solves real problems that consumers have, the chances of success are sky high.

Ephesians 1:11

[11] *In Him also we have obtained an inheritance, being predestined according to the purpose of Him who works all things according to the counsel of His will.*

Prayer

Heavenly Father, I ask that your 'why' becomes my 'why'. As I yield the vision to you, ay your spirit lead me and guide me into all truth, in order to fulfill your mission on this earth. I pray that I would not allow selfishness to block the vision that you have given me. Lord, allow my mission statement to speak of your divine purpose for my business. In Jesus name I pray.

CHAPTER TWO

Determining Your Target Market

I always reiterate that determining and understanding your target market is key to developing and growing your business. In many of my speaking engagements, I often get the question, "How do I determine my target market?" A business determines its target market by the consumers that are likely to need its product. If your business is the production of candy, your target market would definitely be spread across the younger demographics in whatever city you are in. To build a solid foundation, you must first identify your typical customer and tailor your marketing approach accordingly. I have never gone wrong using this approach and I can list several corporations who adopt this approach. It is simply an inevitable part of setting up your business and growing it into a million-dollar brand. Determining your target audience does not mean excluding people who might not need your products, but it is more about channeling your target marketing to better focus on your specific market. With a clearly defined target audience, it is much easier to determine where and how to market your business. Target marketing is a concept that has been a biblical principle and a typical example can be found in the New Testament in the book of Mathew, Chapter 10. Jesus instructed his disciples to target their ministry just like he does and this was not done to reject people. On the other hand, it made Jesus Christ's ministry more effective when he employed 'Target Evangelism' without being prejudiced. Peter and Paul were both apostles who employed Target Evangelism. Paul targeted his ministry to the Gentiles, while Peter channeled towards the Jews. The competitiveness of modern markets in business now makes having a well-defined target market more important than ever. Given that no one can afford to target everyone, small businesses can have a lifeline by targeting their niche market.

A few years ago, we had challenges in our transportation division. It was like running around in circles, and as the business owner, it certainly worried me. We were overspending money in marketing and sales. So, I called my team together, and we started analyzing what could have gone wrong or what we were not doing right. After a few analyses, we discovered that our approach to targeting potential clients was flawed. We realized that we were targeting a wider group of customers instead of focusing on a niche and well-defined target. After re-defining our target clients and separating them by classifying them as Personal Clients, Commercial Clients, and Organization groups, we were able to cut cost and increase profit. To establish your target market, you should research the potential buying audience for your product. Your potential buying audience varies according to the business you are setting up. For example, in an online business, it could range from millions of people or it could be a selected exclusively, depending on the nature of the business.

In a consumer market, it is advisable to narrow down the potential customer base to a defined demographic group. This makes your business more attractive to investors and also helps you in compiling a sales and marketing plan. Examine your business product or modem and discover the most likely consumer through your analysis. Then, define the age range, gender, marital status, and income level of your most likely consumer. Your marketing should be centered on explaining the motivations for buying the product or service. Is it a necessity or luxury? What value does it bring? (Refer to chapter 1). Guessing or assuming would be disastrous, so this research is highly necessary. It can be through questionnaires, surveys, or secondary research, but this exercise is a crucial part of establishing your business and keeping it afloat in a highly competitive market.

Your target market are the customers that are likely to buy from you, and when your marketing is narrowed down to them, it yields better results. As an owner of multiple businesses, this principle has been key to the sustained growth of my various businesses. Resist the temptation of being too general in the hopes of catching a bigger slice of the market. Consider yourself a sniper; would you rather fire 10 bullets in random directions or aim at a specific target? Describe with as much detail as you can based on your knowledge of your product and service. Use family and friends in visualization exercises to get different perspectives. The more the better for your research exercise. Years ago, business owners tended to market their products to 18-49-year olds. That is now history, as the approach would not work anymore. The consumer marketplace has become so differentiated that such generalizations simply cannot work. It would be a huge misconception to generalize the potential market. In the business world today, social-economic status, gender, region, lifestyle, or technological sophistication serve as the index.

Generational marketing, which categorizes customers not just by age, but also by social, economic, demographic, and psychological factors, has been used since the past three decades to derive a clearer picture of target market. As a Christian, the Bible is God's Word to man. In other words, humans were the target market of the Bible. God approves anyone who humbles himself and treasures God's Word. Each book of the Bible, divinely inspired, was written to a specific audience in a specific historic context. The Book of Mathew is a brilliant example of target market in the Bible. Matthew was a Jew writing to the Jews; he constantly referred to the Old Testament's prophecy because the people were familiar with it. This was the best way to fulfill the purpose, which is to link Jesus to the fulfillment of those well-known scriptures. Compare this to the writings of Luke, a Greek Physician whose forte was to write an orderly history of the ministry of Jesus. His intended audience was much broader and this was reflected in the detailed nature of his gospel and the book of Acts.

B2C

Having established the above understanding of Target Market, this brings us to the next step, the concept of B2C.

What is B2C in Business or Marketing? B2C or simply put, business-to-consumer, is the type of commerce transaction in which businesses sell products or services to consumers. Conventionally, this could refer to individuals shopping for clothes at the mall, diners eating in a restaurant, or subscribing to pay-per-view TV at home. However, in modern times, B2C refers to the online selling of products or services or e-tailing in which manufacturers and retailers sell their products to consumers over the internet. It is one of the four cornerstones of e-commerce, along with B2B (more on this concept is coming up ahead in this book). B2C is a model that is quite popular and more people are familiar with it. Whenever you purchase an item online for your own use, you have done an e-tail. Any product can be sold through e-tailing or virtual storefronts. This concept was first developed by Michael Aldrich, an English inventor, who connected a television set to a transaction processing computer with a telephone line and coined the term 'teleshopping'.

'B2C' simply implies Business-to-Consumer, which is the commerce between a business and a customer/consumer. Even though the concept of 'B2C' originated from any type of direct to consumer trade or sales, it has further evolved and become associated with the advent of online selling, e-commerce, or e-tailing. E-commerce or e-tailing reached a crescendo significantly in the late 1990s, and the 1998 holiday shopping season had now been tagged the first, "e-tail Christmas." Amazon had surpassed more than $1 Billion sales for the first time. This online boom posed an immediate challenge to brick and mortar business or direct person to person sale. Businesses and services were lost by the online competition of e-tailing.

The direct consequence of this then triggered traditional brick and mortar businesses to establishing their own online presence in a bid to stay competitive. This has fostered more opportunities for consumers to now enjoy the convenience of online ordering, while saving on shipping expenses with certain retailers by picking up or returning orders to the online retailer's brick and mortar stores.

The rapid growth of the internet in the 1990s further impacted the concept of B2C, as hundreds of thousands of domain business names began to register. The potential was heralded earlier on in books like, "*Future Shop: How Technologies Will Change the Way We Shop and What We Buy*" (1992). This book predicted the incoming e-commerce revolution. There were initially some attendant security problems, but when Netscape developed Secure Socket Layers (SSL) – encryption certificates, consumers felt more secured transferring data over the internet. Consumers and web browsers can identify if a site has an authenticate SSL certificate and know if a site can be trusted or not. Secure Socket Layers (SSL) has gone on to become a key component of web and cyber security. E-commerce further rose though the mid-1990s – 2000s with the teeming popularity of sites such as Amazon.com, Zappos, and Victoria's Secret. As a business owner, I have realized the importance of online sales over time, and developed each of my businesses to operate both brick and mortar, as well as online. It is a very vital part of keeping business afloat.

Nowadays, Consumer-based businesses have the need to sell their products online, and it would be rare not to see this. As a business owner who is starting out, aim to be smart and proactive by creating a platform for your business to be sold online. Online shopping has brought a lot of convenience for consumers. Your potential clients can shop for your products from the convenience of their home or from their mobile devices, which will cause your business to thrive. Having a virtual storefront is a must for any serious business owner. Consumers enjoy the ease and convenience and it creates limitless avenues for you to make sales. With an online or virtual storefront, a business might not need a large inventory stocked at all times. This model is ideal for small businesses. However, there are challenges in B2C just like in every sphere of life, but how you surmount the attendant challenges determines the success of your business. The challenges stem from how to best capture the attention of a potential consumer. Websites over the years have become more fancy and flashier all in a bid to create impression and get a consumer's attention.

I stay on top of our B2C game by being intuitive and allowing innovations from team members. Our virtual sites prioritize easy navigation and clarity to make the consumer's job less stressful. The more accessible and usable your online storefront is, the more it determines if an online customer would return or even stay on the site. Sites should be optimized to garner consumer traffic, which makes Search Engine Marketing (SEM) a necessity. When a consumer searches for your business, search engines such as Yahoo, Google, and Bing should draw attention to your business. Web browsers and consumers generally choose websites on the first few pages of their search results after typing a specific keyword or phrase. Without strong Search Engine Marketing (SEM) for your online store or site, your business would be lost in traffic nipped in the midst and you'd risk losing a potential customer or client. Many professionals and businesses employ this method to boost their suite traffic and ultimately their sales.

The second major challenge of 'B2C' is payment processing. SSL encryption helps consumers to know if a site is not compromised, but many are still cautious about presenting their credit/debit cards to businesses. The site might be safe but the place where the credit card information is stored might not be; hence, the hesitation on the consumer's part. This led the Payment Card Industry Security Standards Council (PCI) to create a compliance standard for any company processing credit cards in the year 2004. Services like PayPal perform the payment processing for online vendors and have proven to be quite popular with online shoppers and businesses. PayPal currently manages close to 500 million accounts, and the figures will continue to grow because E-commerce or e-tailing is here to stay. From the early 2000s until now, online sales have grown by over 800 percent and it will only continue to evolve and expand. As a business owner, make this your prerogative and position your business in a way that you can maximize it.

The world is increasingly becoming a global village and the easiest way to meet customers now as a business owner is in their comfort zone. Laptops, tablets, smartphones, and various other mobile devices have become an integral part of the communications structure, so you want to meet the consumer in these places. Social media has become a huge marketing tool and you cannot underestimate the influence it can have on your business. All my businesses have social media pages that are very active and responsive because the world has evolved a great deal since the invention of social media. Twitter, Instagram, Facebook, LinkedIn, Google, and other social media sites have become marketing tools for businesses looking to stir consumer interest. The market for mobile payments is in the trillion figures today, so employing and deploying the best marketing tools in this sphere is a key cog for your business strategy. There are generally five business models of Business-to-Consumer Sales (B2C): Direct Sellers, Online Intermediaries, Advertising Based, Community Based, and Fee Based.

Direct Sellers: This is the most common type of B2C; it is online retail sites where consumers buy products. It is either manufacturers or small businesses that create and sell products, as well as online versions of popular departmental stores, such as Walmart.Com and Macys.com.

Online Intermediaries: They provide access points for buyers and sellers together without owning the product. This is highly popular in the travel industry with sites such as, Expedia, Priceline, and Hotwire.

Advertising Based: This model leverages on high volumes of web traffic to sell advertising, which in turn sells products or services to the consumer. It uses high-quality free content to attract site visitors who then encounter online ads. Examples of these are The Huffington Post and Observer.Com.

Community Based: This approach refers to gathering online communities based on shared interests to help advertisers market their products directly to site users. The best known is Facebook, which helps marketers target ads to people according to specific demographics.

Fee Based: These direct-to-consumer sites charge a subscription fee for access to their content. Publications that offer a limited amount of content for free, but charge for most of it.

B2B

'B2B' refers to Business-to-Business trade, which is the process in which a business makes a trade with another business. It has often been confused with B2C, but they are not the same. Both business concepts, although related, are markedly different. For example, B2B occurs when a food manufacturer purchases salt from a salt producing company. The salt is a raw material for the food manufacturer and the salt manufacturer's product is a necessity. While B2B typically involves professional staff and legal counsel in terms of negotiation, B2C is determined more by the degree of economic implications or information asymmetry. B2B companies represent a significant part of the United States economy—as many as 72% businesses serve other businesses. B2B transactions volume is much higher than B2C because it is mostly a chain supply. In the process of buying a car, there would be many B2B transactions like manufacturer buying tires, or glass for windows before the final B2C sale of the vehicle to you.

B2B has developed a great deal over the years, but despite the good momentum, there have been a few testing waters. The majority of problems stem from online price negotiation and online collaboration, which have not achieved full development. The Boston Consulting Group (BCG) conducted a survey through in-depth interviews with online traders. The report pointed out that with the maturity of the B2B, and the improvement of the price comparison mechanism, pressure on the sellers increase. The survey found that some of the sellers already felt a lot of pressure brought on by the price comparison. The report presented a valuable analysis in the development trend of the B2B market; each party in the B2B market expects a simplification in each trading field. B2B is basically classified into two models: The Vertical B2B model and the Horizontal B2B model.

Vertical B2B Market: Vertical B2B is generally oriented to manufacturing or a business with two directions: Upstream and Downstream. Producers or commercial retailers can have a supply relationship with upstream suppliers, including manufacturers, and form a sales relationship. Dell, for example, works with upstream suppliers of integrated microchips and computer printed circuit boards.

Horizontal B2B: This is the transaction pattern for the intermediate trading market. It concentrates similar transactions of various industries into one place. This provides a trading opportunity for the purchaser and supplier, typically involving companies that do not own the products and do not sell the products. It is a platform that brings the sellers and purchasers together online.

GOVERNMENT ENTITIES / ORGANIZATION

These are bodies and legal entities that engage in commercial activities on the behalf of a government organization owner. Their legal status comes from being part of government stock companies with a state as regular stakeholder. There is generally no standard definition of a government owned organization or state-owned enterprise, although both terms are used interchangeably. The defining characteristics are that they have a distinct legal form and they are established to operate in commercial affairs. Whereas, they may also have public policy objectives, but they are essentially different from other forms of government agencies or state-owned entities created to pursue purely non-financial objectives.

Proverbs 4:5

Get wisdom, Get understanding, Don't forget, nor turn away from the words of my mouth.

Prayer

God of wisdom, please give me the wisdom needed to reach those who need exactly what I have to offer. Give me the strategy needed to draw them and the wisdom to keep them. Also, I ask that you allow me to remain relevant to my industry. In Jesus name!

CHAPTER THREE

Distribution Channel

D istribution channels in business are a chain of businesses or intermediaries. It is the process through which a good or b a d service passes until it reaches the end consumer. In other words, it's the total process that takes place between a seller putting out his product or service and a consumer receiving the product or service. It includes the wholesalers, retailers, distributors, and the internet. A consumer either uses direct channel to purchase from you, or an indirect channel like a wholesaler or retailer. As a Christian setting up a new business, it is noteworthy to realize that God, our creator, effectively used a distribution channel to pass His messages to his people. A typical example is the story of the Israelites during their years in the wilderness. God raised Moses to be his distribution channel of passing his instructions to the people of Israel. The ministry of Jesus Christ also encompasses this business concept with Him choosing the twelve disciples, who all had purposes for being called. With the ultimate purpose to propagate the gospel, the various apostles and disciples were all distribution channels to push the gospel to humanity.

Your job, when you accept Jesus Christ as your Lord and savior, becomes distribution. That is the first calling; and as a Christian,

God employs you as a distribution channel. After being saved, the next task is to distribute the message to others so that they may also be saved. You did not create the gospel, but you are a messenger to deliver the gospel to each ends of the world. As a business owner, you also need a proper distribution channel for your business to reach your potential client or consumer. Understanding your distribution channel and how it works will determine the success of a business venture. A product or service, no matter how good or brilliant it is, would be useless if it can't effectively reach the end user. A distribution channel is the path, by which all goods and services must travel, to reach the intended consumer. This term also refers to the pathway payments made by the end consumer to the original vendor. Distribution channels can be short or long and depend on the amount of the intermediaries required to deliver a product or service.

Goods and services sometimes get to consumers through multiple channels, both a combination of short and long. The increasing number of distribution channels for consumers to find goods and services increases sales for the business owner. However, it can also create a complex system that sometimes makes distribution management difficult. Subsequently, the longer the distribution channel, the less profit a manufacturer makes because of the intermediary charges employed in the sale. Distribution channels might seem endless, but they are broadly categorized into three main types of channels, all of which include a combination of a producer, wholesaler, retailer, and an end consumer. The first distribution channel, is the longest.

The Three-tier System: The adult beverage and wine industry are a perfect prototype of this distribution channel. In the industry, a winery cannot sell directly to a retailer; hence, it operates in the three-tier system. The three-tier system means that the law requires the winery to sell its products to the wholesaler first, who then sells it to a retailer. Lastly, the retailer sells the product to the end consumer.

The second Distribution Channel. model is based on the producer selling directly to a retailer who subsequently sells it to the end consumer. The second channel contains only a single intermediary. Dell, once again, is a great example, as this company largely sell their products to reputable retailers such as Best Buy.

Direct-to-consumer: This is when the producer sells its product directly to the end consumer. An example would be Amazon. Amazon uses its platform to sell kindles directly to its customers. The direct-to-consumer model is also the shortest distribution channel.

As a business owner, your distribution channel determines how fast and how well your products will sell. Therefore, a thorough analysis of competition is required to decide the best distribution channel that works for your products or services.

Choosing the perfect distribution channel is a pivotal decision for your business growth. What you choose and how you choose it determines how your products are handled and the speed in which they are delivered. Just as Jesus Christ chose each disciple for a reason, businesses choose their distribution channels according to what suits them. A good product or service can be marred by a wrong distribution channel. The distribution channel you choose determines how your products will be handled and the speed in which they will be delivered. Some of the factors to be considered includes: Type of Product, Market, and a Middleman.

Type of Product: If your product is perishable, then you require the fastest means possible to distribute it to the end consumer. Hence, a direct distribution mentioned would be the best bet for such a business owner.

Market: This is the consumer base. Retailers are essential in the distribution method; whereas, business markets may need another approach that you will need to identify based on the type of business.

Middlemen: Middlemen are required depending on your needs and the demands you have. A middleman helps to distribute products quickly and efficiently and is worth it if there are no budget constraints.

Countless business owners erroneously consider their marketing campaign before deciding the distribution channel. I recommend marketing comes in after making a decision on your distribution channel because marketing is the strategy you use to reach your distribution channel. Furthermore, much of your wholesale business depends highly on which method you select as a pathway to reach your consumers/customers. For instance, if you choose to use a sales force as your primary means of reaching people, much of your focus will be on training your sales force to position your product/service effectively. You would need to hire a workforce, coach them, and equip them with key messages. Alternatively, if you choose to reach people through direct mail, then you would focus on obtaining reliable contact lists and setting up staffing call-centers. The smartest business owners identify the distribution channel that works best for their product and services, and then leverage their marketing on this. The distribution channel you employ decides the speed and effectiveness of your products/services getting to the consumers/ customers. Using the wrong distribution channel could be fatal for a business owner, especially a new business owner.

Another important factor to consider when deciding on distribution channel is taking a proper look at competition. You have to study what your competitors are doing and what distribution channel they are using–more importantly, why they are using the distribution channel. Find out if there is a qualitative advantage over other channels or if it is simply because it is the way the industry has always operated. Is there a distribution channel that your competition has overlooked due to stereotypes or status quo? If there are such distribution channels that work and have been neglected, you can gain an advantage on your competitors, by using such distribution channels. If a direct competitor typically uses huge brand retail houses to distribute their products, take advantage of direct sales through the internet; therefore, approaching it from a unique angle. This strategy can give you a massive head start on your competitors as you launch a new business.

You can evaluate a new distribution channel or improve your channel marketing/management at any time. It is especially important to think about distribution when you are going after a new customer segment, releasing a new product or looking for ways to aggressively grow your business. Evaluate how your end-users or consumers need to buy; your chosen distribution channels should deliver the information and service your prospective consumers need. Consider consumers in 'How' and 'Where' they prefer to buy. Does your product need personalized education and training? Do consumers need an additional product to use along with yours? Does your product need installation? Does it need to be serviced? These are pertinent questions that will help you solve the riddle of the best distribution channel for your product or service. To grow beyond direct models, look for companies that already have a relationship with your consumers. Any consultant, wholesalers, or retailers that already have a reach to your customer base should be your natural partners.

When you choose the right distribution channel that works for your products/services, creating all the support systems that work with it is time-consuming and expensive. In the beginning, you orientate your entire work staff in a certain direction and once that is done, it is difficult to reverse your decision. Furthermore, the actual act of building an infrastructure to support a selected distribution channel is also expensive and time-consuming. It is always best to weigh the financial implications that are associated with each and every one of your options in distribution. It is imperative to consider the costs and benefits to the corresponding distribution channel before embarking on it. The cost implications and affordability determine the sustainability of each distribution channel and as a business owner, you ought to be mindful of this. Do you have the required budget to embark on the distribution channel that you believe works for your business? Does employing that distribution channel make your product pricier? These are vital questions that would need to be answered by you, the business owner. Weigh every distribution option thoroughly on this scale before jumping on it.

After assessing and examining the different distribution channel methods available to your business, rank them on an order or scale of preference. The order of preference should be according to what will net you the most amount of revenue at the end of each business year. You may also find that using one distribution channel does not necessarily preclude you from adding more channels as more capital accrue. Some distribution channels might end up being complimentary to each other, and that synergy would make your business more effective and productive. The important step is to carefully consider your options and thoroughly assess them before committing to it. Avoid the temptation of using a particular distribution channel because it is the industry standard or most convenient avenue for your business. Think outside the box from your competition, and discover the best distribution channel that works for your business. If you question the reason for your decision early on, you may discover an overlooked advantage or drawback.

Multimillion-dollar businesses have multiple distribution channels that are mutually exclusive of each other, as well as complimentary to the chain. Distribution channels are a key element of your entire marketing strategy.

Matthew 14:18

He said, "Bring them here to me."
Spirit of the living God, you said to ask and we shall receive.
So I ask that you bless our plan to distribute through every channel of distribution you have allowed me to gain within my industry. I pray that you allow all channels to flow with a spirit of excellence. Amen.

CHAPTER FOUR

Customer Relationship

Customer relationships are highly crucial to the growth and sustenance of any business venture. It is tempting as a business owner to concentrate on making new sales or pursuing new customers, but dedicated attention to existing customers is very important. No matter how small a customer or consumer is, having a good relationship with them is essential for business thriving. The secret to repeat business is following up in a way that has a positive effect on the customer. Customer relationship is the development of an ongoing association between a business owner and a consumer/customer. This relationship is the total sum of marketing communications, sales support, technical assistance, and customer service. Customer relationship is measured by the degree of customer satisfaction through the purchase cycle and after the receipt of goods or service. In plain terms, it is the relationship that a business has with its customers and the way the business treats the customers/consumers. Furthermore, Customer Relationship is the establishment of goodwill between a business and its customers. It requires courtesy, professionalism, and effective response.

A satisfied customer will return to patronize your business again and will also spread the word about your product or services if satisfied. A disgruntled customer is likely not to return to patronize your products/services and would, in turn, tell who cares to listen about the bad experience. Customer relationship comprises of the process and manner by which a business develops, establishes, and maintains relationships with its customer. A business can rise and fall through the support of their customer bases. As a multiple business owner, I realized the efficacy and importance of good customer relationships a long time ago and it has been a benchmark for my business forays. Consequently, I make sure to harp on this point at any speaking engagement or during business coaching. It is absolutely essential that you develop effective customer relations. On a practical level, customer relationship is communicating with your customers effectively and promptly addressing complaints by treating them as opportunities for improvement. In other words: *Listen to your customers.* On a more strategic level, placing the customer at the center of all your business activities, from design, quality, and pricing is a central component of effective customer relationship.

As a business owner, you need to see the world through the eyes of the customer, with them as the focus point, and your role as serving their needs. There are a few ambiguities in understanding customer relationship, as it is different from a personal relationship or a one-time transaction relationship.

For instance, buying a sound system from a consumer's outlet would not be called a relationship. The relationship is forged when a business and a customer/consumer have an interaction or transaction done over time. It is a continuous series of synergistic episodes of interaction multiple times. Occasionally having a cup of coffee from Starbucks does not define a relationship, but when you return to Starbucks and order the same coffee again because you enjoyed the ambiance and the environment, the taste, or the method of making the coffee, these factors are what makes it a relationship in business parlance. Relationship with customers begins with effective follow-up immediately after a sale when you tell the customer/consumer, "Thank You" for patronizing your business. It continues when you find out if the consumer was pleased with your product or service. There are several effective ways to follow-up on a customer/consumer and ensure your business is always on their mind.

Knowledge: Let the customer know what you are doing for them. It can be in the form of a mailed newsletter for existing customers or it can be more informal, such as a phone call. Whatever method you choose, the key is to dramatically point out to customers what excellent service or product you are giving them. Some customers may not notice if you do not point it out to them subtly and it is not cocky to tell customers about the work you have done to please them.

Courtesy Notes: I take time out of my busy schedule to personally send some courtesy notes to clients, "It was nice seeing you," or "I was just sitting at my desk ...." etc. Or if I run into old customers at an event, I make sure to personally greet them and even update them on new products that I have.

Personalize Communication: Voice mail and e-mail make it easy to communicate, but a lot of people lose the personal touch because of that. If you have to leave a voice-mail message, let the customer or client know that you want to talk to them personally or that you can go see them in person.

Remember Special Occasions: Send regular birthday cards, anniversary cards, holiday cards, etc to your customers. Gifts are excellent follow-up tools as well and you do not have to spend a fortune to show that you care. Interesting gifts ideas could be in the form of your branded business souvenirs or a gift idea that links to your business, the customer's business, or their recent purchase.

Consider Follow-up Calls Business as Development Calls: When you talk to or visit old clients or customers, you will often find they have referrals to give you, which can lead to new business. These calls bring a personal touch and helps the customer to build more trust in your brand. These calls are also crucial in developing the customer relationship between your business and the consumer/client.

With all that existing customers can do for you, there is simply no reason to neglect them. I have first-hand experienced how good customer relationships have led to more business ventures for me. There is every reason to stay in regular contact with your customers/consumers. Use your imagination and you would think of plenty other ideas that can help you develop a lasting relationship.

CUSTOMER RETENTION STRATEGY

Customer retention is an offshoot of customer relationship, and it is the potential for a business to retain its customers over a specified period. High customer retention means consumers of the products or services tend to return to continue to buy, or in some other way, not defect to another product or service. Smart business generally attempts to reduce customer defections.

Customer retention starts with the first contact a business has with a client or consumer. It carries on throughout the lifetime of a customer relationship and successful retention efforts take this entire life cycle into account. The ability of your business to attract and retain customers/consumers is related not only to the product/service, but also the way it services existing customers. It is the value customers generate as a result of utilizing the solutions and the reputation it creates within and across the market place. Successful customer retention involves more than giving the customers what they expect and generating loyal advocates of the brand might mean exceeding customer expectations.

I always say creating customer loyalty puts customer value, rather than maximizing profits and shareholder value, at the center of business or marketing strategy. The key differentiation in a competitive environment is often the delivery of a consistently high standard of customer service. In the emerging world of Customer Success, retention is a major objective. Customer retention has a direct impact on profitability, research by John Fleming and Jim Asplund indicate that engaged customers generate 1.7 times more revenue than normal customers. This is why as a business owner, your customer retention strategy has to be an ace. Customer retention requires you to really know your customers and it involves more than just access to usage and survey data. Your retention of a customer /client goes a long way to determine the longevity and profitability of your business. What's better than acquiring one new customer? You may want to say, "Acquiring two customers." However, that is not the case, it is actually retaining an existing customer. There are different ways and initiatives that can be used in retaining a current customer, and creating an effective customer retention strategy is a must for your business. From leveraging convenience to prioritizing personalization, there are so many elements you and your business can test today.

Inspire with a Mission: Sometimes a brand inspires loyalty not through tactics and systems, but through what they stand for. For example, TOMS has built their business model around making the world a better place; for every pair of shoes you buy, one is given to the needy. It is called the "One to One Policy".

Empower with Convenience: You can also call this the Starbucks model; the coffee giants have always been innovative with their marketing, especially in acquiring customers. Starbucks focuses on the sounds and smells inside their shops to provide a delightful customer experience. One of their most innovative customer retention moves is the mobile order & pay feature, which helps customers order their coffee before they even get to the shop.

Leverage Personalization: For big brands, coming across as authentic and human can be hectic. Online grocery shopping and self-service scanners are convenient, but customers still like dealing with people. Customer service is still important. Tesco, a company in the UK, uses Twitter as a way of executing this human touch. They show that they care by adding personality to their interactions with customers.

Speak to Your Customers: Don't underestimate the power of one-on-one conversations with your clients, especially if you are running a digital business. Rapid response times solidifies customer retention faster than anything, and also, customer surveys help customers express what they feel. This will help to identify what you are doing right or wrong, and checkmate it before customer churn.

Ramification and Referral Programs: This also works like a treat; some businesses encourage customers to refer their friends with rewards. For example, a business may say, for every friend you refer you get $20 off your next purchase and the friend you refer gets 20% off their first purchase. You can be innovative along these lines in your retention strategy.

Create Distinction Between You and Competition: Apple is the most popular in this regard to their, "Mac vs. PC" ad campaign. Although it generated a lot of dispute, it set Apple apart from their competitors by identifying the kind of consumers who should buy apple products.

Use Experiences to Elicit Positive Feelings: Experiential marketing has long been used as a way for brands to create positive sentiments with their consumers. Coca-Cola is a master at this. They use sports, music, and events to bring consumers closer to the beverage. Look for ways to create positive feelings in the form of new experiences outside of your main products, services, and value propositions.

These are just some of the ways that successful businesses have used to enhance their customer retention strategy. There are many other ways and you can create one according to the peculiarities of your business. Your business just has to have a working business retention strategy.

MEMBERSHIP OPTIONS

A membership model type of business plan is one where consumers/customers pay a recurring fee to access the value an organization creates. It provides the design for different membership levels, revenue sources, marketing activities, events, and conferences. Starting any business can be a really long journey but rewarding when done right. This is even more applicable to starting a membership or subscription-based business. Unlike other businesses, running membership-based business is an entirely different ball game. While traditional business sells a product or service once, they have to keep selling that product to new customers in order to keep making a profit. In membership businesses, the product or service results in regular or monthly income for a seemingly unlimited period of time. Keeping your subscription product or service up to date and keeping customers happy on a consistent basis takes more effort than a traditional business. You have to be constantly on your toes with content that benefits your members. To be successful in a membership-based kind of business, you should always remember the ultimate goal, which is to make your customers happy. If your customers are not happy and successful, then you cannot be either. Member retention should be your number one priority because it is different from selling a 'one-off product.'

With membership business, retention is a big deal; the more members you lose out the back, the lower your profits will be no matter how many new members are coming in the front. I also preach about knowing your audience and what they need. Make sure members stick around by providing them a good reason to stay. You have to sell to them every month, and this means providing them with fresh content and support on a long-term basis. You build real relationships with these people so you need to be sure you are engaging and interacting with them on a regular basis. Also, have a plan for your content as you grow because chances are, if you are running a good model, your business will grow. While that is the ultimate goal, you also need a plan in place to incorporate new members without overlooking long-time members. A big part of success is creating easy content organization and access as your business grows. Your membership is made up of real people and not robots and because of this, you have to adapt to needs if and when they shift. People tend to grow and shift as the years pass by.

This means that the products and services you offer needs to grow and shift along with them. Ask members questions about what they want as they continue to face new challenges in their respective industries. As long as you are flexible with your strategies, you don't mind creating new and engaging content, and you are able to treat your business as something living and active, you will do great. The membership-based model is so unique and basically the good parts of running it boils down to recurring profits and brand loyalty. If you manage both of these things properly, you can run a successful business for years. This can also be the biggest challenge: managing your members and the benefits you are giving them over the long haul. Some of the pros associated with Membership based business includes:

- Recurring revenue with high profit margins
- Continuous traffic to your site

- Customer loyalty and ability to create instantly a great email list
- Referrals that create additional members/revenue

On the other hand, here are some cons associated with running a membership-based business model:

- Giving customers their money's worth
- Retaining memberships over long periods of time
- Maintaining a good reputation with members and their referrals

CUSTOMER SERVICE

Customer service is essentially the assistance and advice provided by a business to the customer and consumers who purchase their products and services. Customer service should be at the heart of every business owner, and the aim should be to provide an exceptional service that leaves the customer feeling valued and respected. A helpful Biblical Principle on which to build a business is found in Luke 6:31, *"Do unto others as you would have them do unto you."* This is the "Golden Rule", and many great businesses use this principle as the foundation for their business. A wise business owner should always treat others as they would like to be treated.

A business that does not think of its customer will not be thought of by its customers. I cannot remember a time when good customer service has failed me in business relations. Good customer service means helping customers efficiently, in a friendly manner. It is necessary to be able to handle issues for customers and do your best to ensure they are satisfied. Providing good service is one of the most important things that can set your business apart from other competitors. I always have it at the back of my mind that my customers must leave happy and this attitude has helped my business and my relationship with my customers flourish.

Customer service is very important because it can make or kill your business dreams; you do not want the ire of an unsatisfied customer. Customer service helps you to increase customer loyalty and increase the amount of money customers/consumers spend with your business. It is the total sum of service that relates to the service you and your staff provide, before, during, and after a trade transaction. I believe how I interact with my customers and improve my customer service skills leads to greater satisfaction for my customers.

I try to make the experience as enjoyable as possible for them and so does my staff. No matter the size of your business, customer service needs to be the focal point for it to be successful. Although, it might take extra resources, time, and money, good customer service leads to customer satisfaction and that is invaluable. This generates positive word-of-mouth for your business and keeps your customers and consumers happy.

When the customer is happy, it encourages them to purchase your product and services again and your business will grow.

Good customer service will enable you to stand out from your competition. It helps you maintain a positive reputation among potential customers/consumers and encourages existing customers to buy from you again. It is six times more expensive to acquire a new customer than to retain an existing customer. Some of the reasons why customer service is very important are listed below:

- It increases customer loyalty.
- It increases the amount of money each customer spends with your business.
- It increases the frequency a customer patronizes your business.
- It generates positive word-of-mouth about your business.
- It decreases barriers between a business and customers

Exceptional customer service skills comprise the following:

- Treating your customers respectfully.
- Following up on feedback.
- Handling complaints and returns gracefully.
- Understanding your customers' needs and wants.
- Exceeding customer expectations.
- Going out of your way to help them.

Ephesians 6:7-8 ESV

Rendering service with a good will as to the Lord and not to man, knowing that whatever good anyone does, this he will receive back from the Lord, whether he is a slave or free.

Prayer

Father, I thank you for the many customers you are going to send my way. I ask that you give me the words to say in order to serve our amazing customers. Lord, grant me the wisdom to deal with all types of personalities and attitudes. Give me the grace to serve in Jesus name. Amen!

CHAPTER FIVE

Revenue Stream

Revenue stream is simply another name for income. It has become the general business parlance in the business world. This was borrowed from investment talk where assets are said to have a, "future revenue stream". It is considered a better terminology than sales, taxes, salary, and more. The phrase has come into current use in business to mean sales. More specifically, it is often qualified by modifiers, such as "new" or "additional". Thus, gradually taking on a distinct and specialized meaning in certain contexts to mean a new, novel, undiscovered, potentially lucrative, innovative, and creative means of generating income or exploiting potential. The phrase also comes in handy in an internet age where revenue is sometimes generated in modern ways different from old-fashioned across the counter sale. The concept of Revenue Streams encompasses the various sources from which a business earns money from sale of products or provision of services. Types of revenues your business earns depends on the types of activities carried out by your business. Analyzing your business' performance in terms of revenue is a highly important task for you as a business owner.

Personally, I try to recognize the different revenue streams from which my businesses generate cash and interpret the revenue figures on financial statements. My accounting team works closely with me on revenue numbers to reflect the amount by the business when sales are made. Irrespective of whether the cash has been received at that time, it is recorded as an earning. In business, revenue stream is generally made up of either recurring revenue, transaction- based revenue, project revenue, or service revenue. According to Dooley, "the revenue of a business is its sales, receipts or income." In government, the term "Revenue Stream" often refers to different types of taxes. When your revenue stream is well documented, it aids you in planning, in business strategies, and as an investment. Every business wishes to generate new revenue, and the vital ingredient in the creation of new revenue streams remain perennial and ancient. Individual creativity and enterprise are two characteristics that have driven discerning entrepreneurs to the greatest heights.

Revenue streams are often created by people who are more than simply threatened by change or fascinated by the new. Your eyes need to be open to see opportunities that can increase your revenue streams. You also need the discipline and skill to turn ideas and notions into actual salable products and services. Small businesses have been particularly active in the creation of the digital age. Virtually, every big-name corporation began as one or a pair of creative people. They foresaw and acted and consequently created what amounts to more than a stream, a revenue fountain. The quest for new streams of revenue is stimulated by change and it can either be a positive or negative change. United States business history is documented with the discovery of endlessly new revenue streams in response to technological advancements. The buzz about new revenue streams surrounding the internet is a vivid example. Change creates opportunities and as a business owner, the ability to see a potential and exploit it, is what creates new revenue streams for your business.

Change may hurt or entice, but, either way, effective innovation makes use of the stimulus. A classic example of positive stimulus is the appearance of home computers and the invention of joy-sticks to enable kids and adults to play games on the computer. Games, joy-sticks, and visual interfaces and pointer devices all produced massive global revenue streams and stimulated others. Interesting innovations by institutions facing income problems show how these institutions are coping with change on the negative side. For instance, public television was once wholly funded by the government, but it was forced to eventually develop fund-raising skills when government funding abated. Museums seeking additional revenue have developed lucrative new revenue streams like memberships and establishing very attractive specialized retail activities. Some of the activities include selling art objects, souvenirs, books, music, toys, and more. Some museums even venture beyond the museum walls and have established retail outlets in malls. As a business owner, the ability to observe and sense a potential revenue stream would make you stand out from competitors.

The ability to spot the potential and tap into it would give you a serious head start over competition. A successful business does not rely on just one product or service, it relies on multiple sources of income or revenue streams. As a business owner and a Believer, model your life after Jesus Christ. Jesus Christ did not only rely on his disciples to spread the gospel, but he recruited multiple streams of people to also propagate the gospel. In totality, revenue stream is all the sources that brings money into your business. However, there are different types of revenue streams; at the highest level of business, there are operating and non-operating revenues. Operating revenues describe the amount earned from the core business operations of your business operations. Sales of product and services is an example of operating revenue. Non-operating revenues refer to the money earned from the side activities of your business. Typical examples are interest revenue and dividend revenue.

There are hundreds of different revenue streams that businesses use in various industries, but for the purpose of this book we will look at the main types of revenue streams for any business.

REVENUE FROM PRODUCTS, SALES, OR SERVICE FEES

This is the core operating revenue stream for most businesses. It is usually specified as sales or service revenue, depending on if your business is a product or a service.

Interest Revenue: This type of revenue is a non-operating revenue stream; it records interest earned on investments such as debt owed and the likes.

Rent Revenue: This is also a core operating revenue stream for major businesses across different industries. It is the amount earned from renting out buildings or equipment and it is classified as a non-operating revenue.

Dividend Revenue: This is the proceeds earned from holding stocks of other companies and it is also a non-operating revenue.

Now that we have established what Revenue Stream is and the different types, I will take you through a few examples of revenue streams in the business world. Revenue streams categorize the earnings your business generates from certain pricing mechanisms and channels. Simply put, a revenue stream can take the form of one of the following revenue models.

Transaction Based Revenue: This is the proceeds from sales of products that are mostly one-time customer payments.

Service Revenue: This refers to revenue generated by providing a service to customers/consumers and calculated based on time. A typical example of this is my business coaching classes.

Project Revenue: Project Revenue is earned through one-time projects either with new or existing customers.

Recurring Revenue: Recording Revenue refers to the income from ongoing payments for continuous or after-sales services to customers/consumers. This model is the most commonly used by businesses because it is predictable and it assures the business's source of revenue as ongoing. There are many types of recurring revenue streams that include subscription fees (Netflix, iTunes), renting or leasing assets, licensing content to third parties, brokerage fees, as well as advertising fees.

When you have mastery of the revenue streams for your business, it enables you to plan business strategies effectively. It also helps you to maximize untapped potential for your business and create a unique marketing strategy for the business.

METHOD OF PAYMENT

What is method of payment in Business Parlance? Method of payment is defined by the Business Dictionary as the way that a buyer chooses to compensate the seller of a good or service that is also acceptable to the seller. In other words, method of payment is the way your potential customer/consumer chooses to pay for the products or service you are rendering that is acceptable to your business. Common payment methods used in modern business include cash, checks, credit or debit cards, money orders, bank transfers, and online payment services like PayPal, Venmo and Cashapp. I always consider the method of payment I will offer when starting a new business and review them regularly. This enables me to see if I will be keeping up with my customer's payment preferences or if I will be meeting their needs. In the same vein, this should be a key point for you when starting your business. It is an important step to ensure the management of cash flow in your business is effective. The payment method you choose determines the facilities your business would require.

Credit and Debit Card Payments: A credit card allows consumers to pay for goods and services by incurring a debt with a credit card provider. On the other hand, debit cards deduct the amount of money from a sale to a customer's bank account.

Direct Debit Payments: This requires already having an established business. Direct payments are fast and funds are usually in your account by 9:00 AM the next business day. However, beware of fees to process direct debit payments.

EFTPOS Payments: This popular method is referred to as, "Pos", especially in sub-Saharan Africa. EFTPOS means Electronics Funds Transfer at The Point of Sale. This method of payment allows customers to pay directly into your bank account with a bank card as well as a credit or debit card.

Online Payments: Online payment services like PayPal enables your customers to pay for purchase of products or services through your website. Payments may be automatic and convenient, but make sure to use encryption for sending payment information to protect your customer/consumers from cyber criminals.

Cash Payment: This has been in existence since taking over from trade by barter. Cash payments are useful for low value items or if other payment methods are unavailable. It requires you tracking your sales through a cash register. This method also requires you to visit the bank often to deposit your cash to reduce the risk of theft.

Check: Paying by check has become less frequent since the advent of various electronic payment options discussed above. Checks also require higher levels of handling to process them and can attract fees. It also takes about three days for the funds to clear.

Money Order Payments: A money order tells a bank, credit union, building society, or post office to pay you money. Unlike Checks, money orders are prepaid and cannot bounce due to other problems such as suspected fraud.

Gift Cards and Vouchers: This can increase sales around special occasions such as Christmas and birthdays. It also helps to promote your brand while bringing in new customers. In some cases, gift cards are only valid for a limited period and businesses will need to honor it in that time frame.

Bitcoin and Digital Currencies: This is the latest form of payment symbolized by the explosion of the digital world. Digital currencies are similar to money in usage to buy and sell products and services. However, businesses do not have to accept digital currency as payment as it is not yet a legal tender.

Each payment method has different advantages and disadvantages and no one type of payment method is the best. As a matter of fact, various businesses make use of multiple payment methods, such as the ones discussed above. However, I advise choosing payment methods according to the needs of your business. When choosing payment methods, consider how their advantages or disadvantages affect your customers and business operations. Cash can be anonymous and reliable, but it is also very expensive to handle and has the huge risk of theft. EFTPOS is quick and has a lower risk of theft, but requires a fee for the service. So, it boils down to you analyzing what works best for your customers and your business.

Some of the factors that you need to consider in choosing a payment method for your business are:

Customer Preference: Choosing a payment method your customer prefers will ensure prompt payments. The most common means is through credit or debit card.

Risk: Cash, for example, has a higher risk of theft since it is physical and it also carries the huge risk of mistakes in calculation.

Privacy: Some payment methods are more private than others. Credit cards, for instance, automatically record transactions. Some customers might prefer to pay cash for certain goods and services like medications for privacy reasons.

Service Fees: EFTPOS and credit card service providers charge service fees.

Transaction Costs: Banks may charge a cost for each transaction made.

Reliance on Electrical and Telecommunications Infrastructure: EFTPOS, as a case study, uses electricity and requires access to a phone network. Payment can be unavailable if systems go down or work slow.

PERCENTAGE OF CONTRIBUTIONS TO OVRERALL REVENUE

The percentage of revenue of a business is the act that allows your business to record costs and profits for a particular period of time, mostly quarterly. It can also be a six-months period or fiscal business year. The percent of revenue relies heavily on estimated gross profit and total cost calculations to determine quarterly profits and expenses. According to BusinessDictionary.com, this is most useful when a business can reasonably predict the profits and costs for its running. To determine cumulative revenue, multiply the cost incurred to date with total production. Divide the resulting number by the total estimated cost of sale to obtain cumulative revenue. For instance, a business that incurs $10,000 in cost for a contract worth $50,000 and estimates $30,000 in total completion costs, would have a cumulative revenue for the given period of time as $16,666.

Deuteronomy 8:18

Any you shall remember the Lord your God for it is He who gives you power to get wealth that He may establish His covenant which He swore to your fathers as it is this day.

Prayer
Jehovah
Jireh

You are the Lord who provides all things for your children. Dear Heavenly Father, please release the power to get wealth into my life. Give me your mind to make the right decisions on how to manage the revenue you release. In Jesus name. Amen!

For a business with a long-term contract to provide goods and services, use the percentage of revenue or completion method as a means to track expenses and earnings over multiple financial quarters. This makes preparing tax documents easier because the company is not waiting until completion date to calculate expenses and total earnings.

CHAPTER SIX

Key Resources

K ey resources are the main inputs that your business uses to create its value proposition, service customers, and deliver products to consumers. As a business owner, take your key resources very seriously and ensure they flow optimally. Mathew 6:21 says, *"Where our treasure is, there is where your heart is."* The key resources of your business are the components of your "Treasure" (The Business). Key resources are the most important things you need to make your business model run. Business models are usually based on tangible or intangible resources. Key resources are the main assets of your business that you use to create the end product or service. It is usually differentiated from the key resources being used by your competition. This business term encompasses the operational end of the business spectrum and dictates what you need, the materials you use, the equipment required, and the types of people you need to employ. Every business has key resources and it is through them that you generate value propositions and revenues.

Key resources bring your value proposition to life for your chosen customer segment and defines the barest minimum required to deliver to your customers/consumers. The business model you embark highly determines the type of key resources you need.

A software developing business will have human resources as the key resource. On the other hand, a manufacturing business would consider production hardware as key resources. This concept is directly relevant to the number and type of key activities that your business engages in. In the long run, the quality of your key resources impacts the sustainability and profitability of your business. For example, if your business doubles sales in a year and grows beyond expectations, how do you handle such growth? It is by recognizing your key resources and what impact the rapid growth would have on them with the increased demand. Understanding your key resources is how you determine if your physical resources are enough for the growth or if you require additional resources investment. Similarly, you would know if your current human resources will suffice or if additional talent is needed.

Have a clear purpose. Ephesians 2:10 says, *"You are God's workmanship who has been created to do good words that God has prepared in advance."* I try to find the gifts and passions of my team members to inspire them. When a business seeks to know the passions of its staff, higher productivity is subsequently guaranteed. Passionate people are reliable people so you would want to fuel those passions that could drive your business to great heights. Key resources can be classified into four main types: physical, intellectual, human, and financial resources. Furthermore, a business has the option of leasing its key resources or owning them, as well taking on key partners who would provide access to these resources.

Physical Resources: This terminology describes the tangible resources that your business uses to create value proposition. These can be any equipment, inventory, buildings, manufacturing plants, and distribution networks that enable your business to function. For instance, my car rental business: The cars are the physical resources that enable the business to run. Likewise, a microchip manufacturing business like Intel needs semi-conductor plants as a key resource. Without such adequate infrastructure available, the business would fail to innovate to keep up with customer/consumer demands.

Intellectual Resources: This type of resources is mostly non-physical and intangible like patents, IP, copyrights, and even partnerships. Customer lists, customer knowledge, and even your staff represent a form of intellectual resource. Intellectual resources require a great deal of time and expenditure to develop. However, once developed, they can offer unique advantages to your business. Sportswear manufacturer, Adidas, is heavily dependent on their brand to sell products to a customer segment that is devoted to the brand. Similarly, Adobe and Microsoft rely on software that have been tweaked and perfected over years of trial and error. Some businesses rely mostly on intellectual resources and a business such as Google is currently buying a patent library from Nortel to boost intellectual resources.

At the turn of the millennium, business owners have increasingly realized the significance of intellectual resources. This is evident in the increase of patents being filed in the United States. Apple's patents grew by 68% between 2011 and 2012. In the dame period, Google's patent grew by 170%. Patents have become increasingly a major driver of this company's business and growth, with intellectual resources being a key resource.

Human Resources: Employees are the most important assets of any business organization. Yet, a lot of business owners easily overlook their assets. Human resources are pivotal in business, especially in the service industry or businesses that require a great deal of creativity and an extensive knowledgeable pool.

Financial Resources: Financial resources include cash, credit lines, and the ability to have stock option plans for employees. Every business has key resources in finance, but some have stronger financial resources than others. A wealth management business like a bank's existence is based entirely on the availability of this key resource. Likewise, an insurance business will sell insurance policies worldwide, but if it does not have sufficient capital, it would fold up. Sufficient capital is needed to cover various insurance claims and an insurance business without solid capital would not survive in the market. A car manufacturing business may require physical resources, such as assembly robots or intellectual resources. They also provide customers the option of buying or leasing. This can give customers more options, such as better loan terms instead of those offered by banks or other financial institutions.

The quality and nature of your business's key resources command how well you will fulfill your value proposition. If the value proposition is longevity and sustainable quality, you can still cater to customer segment that cannot outright afford your product by availing financing options. This ensures that both the customer segment that can afford your product or service, and the ones that cannot afford it, will still patronize you.

KEY RESOURCES IN RELATION TO TYPES OF BUSINESS

Business models are generally categorized into three categories in the business world. All three categories have businesses with similar key resource requirements. The three business model categories are:

- Product Driven Businesses
- Scope Driven Businesses
- Infrastructure Driven Businesses

Product Driven Businesses: These are businesses that focus on the creation and sale of a product. Every product has its unique characteristics and an eager customer segment willing to purchase it.

Scope Driven Businesses: These are businesses dedicated to providing a value proposition to a particular customer segment. A business aiming to specialize in providing information technology expertise to a law firm would fall under a Scope Driven Business. This business has key resources in the well-developed intelligence about the target customer segment.

Infrastructure Driven Businesses: As the name implies, these achieve profitability through leveraging their developed and implemented infrastructure. The telecommunications industry invests heavily in developing the telecommunications infrastructure in a country, and then reaps the rewards for years. Retailers are also an example of infrastructure driven businesses because they depend primarily on their established infrastructure to sustain their profitability in the long-term.

Leaders are called to lead with passion and as a business owner, you are the leader of the team. A leader in business is called upon to make many investments and that honor falls on you. You must make use of the resources of your business to make the right investments in the business, people, and infrastructure. When resources are harnessed effectively, business will grow. Good investment and adequate resources will grow a business and set the direction and path to success and ensure growth and development. When evaluating what their key resources should be, many business owners fail to think strategically. Some come up with generic resources that would be common in any business in the industry they are operating in.

It is imperative to do an evaluation of each key resources discussed above and compare whether the resources mentioned is essential for the success of your business. Talented human resources are a necessity for most businesses, but one needs to ponder on whether they form the very building block upon, which the success or failure of the company depends on. No business can ever exist unless it has certain resources to support it. Even a freelancer running a business alone still requires financial and physical assets, such as a bank account, a space to work, internet connection, and a website, etc.

COST OF RESOURCES

Cost of resources describes the most important costs incurred while operating your business and value proposition. Creating and delivering value, maintaining customer relationships, and generating revenue, incur costs. Cost of Resources is the cost of all the elements used in carrying out your business activities, including elements such as workers' salaries and the cost of materials. Such costs can be calculated by easily identifying your key resources, key activities, and key partnerships. Some businesses generally require more costs than others depending on the nature and key resources. Naturally, every business owner wants to minimize cost, but low-cost structures are more important to some business models than to others. Therefore, cost of resources can be classified into two categories depending on the business model. The two categories are: Cost-Driven and Value-Driven. Many business types fall in between these two broad categories.

- Cost-Driven: These business models focus on minimizing costs wherever possible; the approach aims at creating and maintaining the leanest possible cost on key resources. They use low price value propositions, maximum automation, and extensive outsourcing. Typical examples are no-frills airlines, such as Southwest, Spirit, and EasyJet, which are cost driven airlines.

- Value-Driven: Some businesses are less concerned about the cost implications of a particular business model design and instead focus on value creation. Premium Value Propositions and a high degree of personalized service usually characterize value-driven business types. A luxury hotel with its plush facilities would fall under this category. Understanding the key resources for your business and how it works would help you to minimize cost and accelerate your business growth.

2 Corinthians 9:8

8 And God is able to make all grace abound toward you, that you, always having all sufficiency in all things, may have an abundance for every good work.

Prayer

Lord, I know that all things come from you. You own the cattle on a thousand hills. So there is nothing on this earth that is not given to me. I pray for you resources to be released into my business and my family. Father, I ask this by faith in Jesus name. Amen!

CHAPTER SEVEN

Key Partners

Key partners are the network of suppliers and partners that make your business work. Businesses form strategic partnerships to optimize their business models, reduce risk, and or acquire resources. Look at the key partnership you may need to make your business thrive. Key partnerships are strategic to the success of your business. The concept of partnership was rooted in the Bible way before it became a business parlance, "Key Partners", "Partnership", and "Partners." Partnership was established from the doctrine of the Tri-unity or Trinity. God reflects partnership with the Godhead (The Father), The Son (Jesus Christ), and the Holy Spirit as a perfect model of partnership. This doctrine permeates the whole scriptures from the beginning to the end. See (Gen. 1:26-27); Matt. 28:19, John 14:26 and Rev. 1:4-5. Our Christian journey itself is a partnership, as God calls us into a vertical partnership with Him by winning souls for the Kingdom. God calls us into partnership with Him in order to fulfill His plans for the world's redemption.

Similarly, a Christian entrepreneur needs key partners to provide its value proposition to its customer segment. A business partnership occurs when two business entities form an alliance, which may either be a really loose relationship where both parties retain their independence. It can also be to form more partnerships or an exclusive contract which limits the two companies to only that business relationship. As I mentioned earlier, when I first started my entrepreneurship journey, my goal was initially to make me (Rudy) successful. But then, I slowly realized that one cannot go far without key partnerships. When I started a towing vehicle business, I knew it was a good business, but I needed to find someone who had the experience and made him my partner. I did the same with my hair salon business, as well as my other business. Identifying key partnerships accelerated my business growth. Partnerships are not only in-person, remote key suppliers that you can establish a relationship with for your business growth are also key partners.

I used to own a hospice where we would take care of patients for a month before the government paid us. I had to partner with key businesses, such as pharmacies. They also got paid when I got paid by the government, and the same goes for the equipment supply companies I partnered with to supply all equipment needed. I partnered with them, instead of seeking capital to buy larger equipment. Partners and partnerships in business can be classified into four different types: Strategic Alliances, Co-opetition, Joint- Ventures, and Buyer-Supplier Relationships.

Strategic Alliances: This type of partnerships are between non-competitor businesses. An example is when a business such as a news agency supplies news to both online and offline channels. Barnes & Noble and Starbucks are perfect examples. Literary fans describe perfect reading moments as reading on a rainy day, curled up on a sofa with a cup of tea or coffee.

This makes the coupling of a bookstore and coffee company a perfect alliance.

Co-opetition: There can also be a strategic partnership between the same business fields. Such partnerships help spread the risk both companies may take and helps when both try to do something new. It can also mean a confirmed supply stream. A mobile phone company needs earth metals to manufacture their phones, so securing the supply of rare earth metals can be a reason to form a strategic partnership with competitors.

Joint-Ventures: Another type of partnership is when a joint venture is more developed in regards to starting a new business. Both partners can have a mutual interest in developing a new business, possibly due to the emergence of a new market or access to new geographic area. Both businesses can opt for such an option if they both provide some input into the business. Hence, a Dutch company that specializes in producing cheese might choose to go into a joint venture with a milk producing local company, to start making cheese in a new region.

Buyer-Supplier Relationships: These are the most popular types of partnerships. It assures that you have a reliable source of supplies coming in, and for your supplier, this means they have a steady confirmed buyer for their product.

Partnerships have been established right from the olden days in the Bible and permeates every aspect of our society today. In business, partnerships are especially important because key partners facilitate business development and growth; however, there are very important things to keep in mind to form an alliance.

Right Partnership Agreements: Whether your partnership is with a business or an individual, it is highly important for the relevant parties to have clear partnership agreements drafted, along with legal counsel.

Defining Expectations: Often times, new businesses fail to establish their expectations from the outset, leading to many conflicts later. A Christian business owner needs to ensure that he has shared his expectations openly with his partner and vice versa from the beginning.

Impact on Clients: In forming a partnership, it is crucial to evaluate your value proposition and your key resources, and to make sure your partner is filling any gaps. This can only be fulfilled by evaluating how the partnership translates or relates to the customer/consumer.

Win-Win Situation: For a partnership to be healthy and sustainable, it has to be a win-win situation for both parties. In other words, there has to be visible gains to both parties, as well as the customer/consumer.

Selecting Partnerships: Some partnerships seem lucrative in theory, but fail to get off the ground practically. Furthermore, changes in the business context may also make some business partnerships irrelevant. In such cases, it is important to end these partnerships quickly to avoid further waste of resources.

There are a myriad of reasons for a business to opt for partnership, but healthy partnerships are very instrumental in making a business a success or a failure. A business can optimize its resource utilization, create new resource streams, or mitigate risks behind major business decisions by taking on a partner before commencing the business. Like the earlier example of the towing business I ventured into, working in the industry gave me an idea of how lucrative the business was. However, I needed someone with actual expertise in towing to make the business work, so partnering up with someone with expertise was the key to that business idea taking off. Your business may partner with a number of other businesses or organizations for different reasons, but not all will help your business. Also, partnerships do change over the course of a business life cycle. The types of partnerships that may be a necessity during the first year of a start-up, differs significantly from the nature of the required partnership in three or four years.

WHY PARTNERS AND PARTNERSHIPS IN BUSINESS?

Partnership is a tricky action that involves a lot of negotiation and an element of trust. There can be varying reasons why a business decides to seek a key partner rather than going solo. There are primarily three reasons attributed to the motivations behind a business seeking key partners or partnerships.

Optimization and Economy of Scale: Most business organizations are heavily focused on the bottom-line and cost-cutting or smart spending. This is a major reason why business owners enter into different types of partnerships. Key partners can help you in efficacy and in optimizing your production chain. It is unrealistic as an entrepreneur to think that you have all the resources to conduct your key activities in-house. Most partnerships can help to share infrastructures or outsource some activities to more cost-effective options. Citroen, Peugeot, and Toyota joined hands to create a small, affordable car for the masses. These cars looked almost the same except for the chassis and few internal and external details.

Reducing Risk and Uncertainty: Having a good relationship with your key partner reduces the inherent risk that comes with doing your own business. You can also guarantee supply to your business rather than being dependent on suppliers who aren't key partners and would therefore not give precedence to your business over others. Many business competitors may form a strategic partnership to share the risk of bringing something new into the market, while still competing in various aspects of the industry. Key partners help reduce the risks that would be undertaken by just one business–this is another reason why businesses seek key partnerships.

Acquisition of Particular Resources & Activities: There are certain things your business may not have internally, which could also require a heavy investment of time and money. Forming an alliance with a key partner who already has these processes and the infrastructure developed comes in extremely handy. Business models can be extensive maps of plenty activities that a business needs to perform or the endless resources required to perform these activities successfully. However, it is rare for a new business venture to have the resources or capabilities in place to fulfill the mandate set down by the business model. Therefore, many new businesses begin their journeys by forming partnerships that give them access to the required resources or processes that they require, but unable to own yet. Many mobile operators partner with IT companies to develop operating systems required, rather than bearing the investment themselves. Bicycle manufacturers get into selective partnerships with bicycle parts manufacturers of their preference, who then customize the parts, such as the color or size of bicycle seats.

KEY BUSINESS PARTNERSHIP

Apple co-founder Steve Jobs famously stated, "Great things in business are never done by one person; they're done by a team of people." Partnerships are key to successful business operations, either internally or externally. Leadership is more than just a science or an art–it is more than a craft. Your ability to look inward and become fully self-aware, as well as the ability to look outward and build an understanding of others is highly expected of you as a business owner. Specifically, you need to meet the needs of people, including employees, managers, directors, colleagues, teams, shareholders, and even external customers and personal connections. These partnerships are key for the success of running a business and maintaining an efficient working relationship requires some savvy. A leader needs to communicate openly and listen more. A leader also needs to be honest with facts, be accountable, and have a dynamic vision.

You also have to be compassionate and empathetic and able to use both emotional and social intelligence to build relationships.

You have to identify the importance of having business partners for your business and develop the right chemistry with them to optimize results. The thinking dynamics, the performance approaches, and ways of connecting to customers have to be aligned. As much as your employees work to meet your demands as the leader, you also have to meet their needs. Your partners will work better when there is a clarity in direction and expectations. In a motivating and supportive way, both the short-term goals and long-term vision need to be carefully articulated in communication. Reasonable and realistic goals within the vision message should be compelling. As a Christian entrepreneur, it is significant to share the company strategies authentically and to get your business partners to believe in it. Your partners look up to you to embrace their strategic responsibilities, and to be fully accountable for their actions. I try to empower my employees in the building of global plans and strategies along with desired metrics.

I manage them, coach, and support the employee population so that each individual can successfully execute the vision and scale obstacles. It is also pertinent as a business leader to show a caring side to your human partners. Demonstrate gratitude and acknowledge achievements and contributions to the business. Through praise and positive kindness, a leader encourages loyalty and commitment to the business. When business partners' engagement and satisfaction is priority, you derive a higher level of retention. Also, value creativity and ingenuity by others as this fosters a culture of learning and development. Help them find joy through self-discovery and build a culture based on win-win solutions. Support the growth and the development of talent for the future.

KEY SUPPLIER PARTNERSHIP

Key suppliers are any party that supplies goods or services is necessary to your creation of value proposition as an entrepreneur. A supplier may be distinguished from a contractor or sub-contractor, who commonly adds specialized input to deliverables. In more straight-forward terms, a supplier is defined as a person, organization, or other entity that provides something that another person, organization, or entity needs. During every transaction, there are suppliers and buyers. Suppliers provide or supply products or services while buyers receive them. In business, every company has at least one supplier supplying the things that makes the business run.

Before heading into a business venture, you need to identify the key suppliers to your line of business and work on creating a partnership with them. When I set up a hospice, the first step I took was to source for key suppliers because that would reduce my overhead cost immensely. I needed equipment supply, medical supplies, and pharmacy supplies, so I struck a partnership with a medical supply company, pharmacy supply, and equipment supply company. Having identified them as being crucial to the success of the hospice, they became the key suppliers for my hospice business. Each company got paid for their services after the government paid me, which ensured a smooth running of the business. Partnering with suppliers to develop a deep and mutually beneficial relationships long-term is a means to lessen risk and develop true supply excellence. Key suppliers are not just companies or a single person. A country can sometimes be a key supplier. Japan, for example, virtually imports all of its oil and gas, and Saudi Arabia is the largest oil supplier. These kinds of relationships between the countries makes Saudi Arabia a key supplier to Japan. Let's imagine you are setting up a bespoke furniture business. The first steps you would want to take are finding a timber company to supply you the wood and also tool makers. The kick-off and success of the business rests squarely on your ability to find these key suppliers and establish the partnership that would propel your business.

Habakkuk 2:2-3

² Then the Lord answered me and said: "Write the vision And make it plain on tablets, that he may run who reads it.³ For the vision is yet for an appointed time; But at the end it will speak, and it will not lie. Though it tarries, wait for it; because it will surely come, it will not tarry.

Prayer

Dear heavenly father, I ask that you send partners who share the same vision as me. Those that will see the ultimate goal, and are willing to work in order to fulfill that mission. In Jesus name! Amen.

CHAPTER EIGHT

Key Activities

K ey activities of a business represent what the business must do to make value proposition work. Every business principle you need to succeed is already in the Bible. It is packed with life lessons, stories of humankind's experiences with God and when carefully examined, you will see some of the most popular business principles in the world today ingrained in it. You need a lot of diligence to establish your key activities in business and to also maximize it. The activities that take place for a business model to work is what is referred to as Key Activities in Business parlance. Diligence means showing care. The Bible says in Proverbs 21:5: *"The Plans of the diligent lead surely to abundance, but everyone who is hasty comes only to poverty."* Your business's key activities must be built carefully according to the business model you employ. These activities can be producing a product or providing a service or a mix of both. For example, if your business focuses on production of a product, your activities may include learning more about the customers and new production techniques to improve your product.

For a chair production business, one of your key activities will be doing market research to find out if customers are happy with your chairs, or if you need to update the model to better fit their needs. If you operate a restaurant, some of your activities may be to experiment on new recipes to provide customers with new dishes or provide more varied options for your customers. In a pumpkin farm, the business owner's key activity will be to produce fresh pumpkin products. However, that would also include activities to experiment on new products that he/she can sell, such as, 'pumpkin wine' or, 'pumpkin jam'. Key activities are the most important tasks a company must carry out in order to fulfill its business purpose, which is your value proposition. To be successful, your business must carry out key actions that are primarily dictated by the business model. Just like key resources, key activities are pivotal in a business fulfilling its value proposition, reaching its customer segments, sustaining customer relationship, and creating long-term revenue streams.

Key activities vary according to the business model employed by you. A business that relies heavily on its third party contracts will list channel management as a key activity. For a product driven business, more significance would be lent to activities such as continuous research to better understand their users, as well as constant innovation in technology. Hence, a key activity for a software business like Microsoft will be Software Development, while Supply Chain Management would be a key activity for a computer manufacturer like Dell. When establishing your key activities, it is essential to take a holistic view of the business and evaluate the related building blocks as well. This will enable you to understand how they will contribute to your key activities. There are pertinent questions to ask based on your value propositions:

- What kinds of activities are key to your business?
- What kinds of activities are key to your distribution channels?
- What kinds of activities are important if we want to maintain our customer relationships?
- What kinds of activities are fundamental to your revenue streams?

The value propositions of a business ultimately determine the kind of key activities the business will undergo. However, as the business flourishes, it may begin to include other activities in this block as well. Creating a bloated product with tons of extra feature that are of no value to your customer, but adds to his investment, should be avoided by all means. A product is a combination of its form and function. By function I mean, defining and detailing exactly what the product does and how it does it. This form is crucial to the customer experience and it helps in determining key activities. Also, the kind of customer relationship you want to establish will entail key activities to bring it to life.

Key activities in the business model are broadly categorized into three different types, which are: Production, Problem Solving, and Platform/Network. (Based on research by two scholars: Charles B. Stabell and Oystein D. Eljeldstad.)

Production: These activities relate to designing, manufacturing, and delivering product in substantial quantities and/or of superior quality. Production activity is typically common to manufacturing firms. The key activities would subsequently be:

- Control of Production
- Manage website, online orders, and distribution of product
- Creating Branding Strategy
- Marketing and Promotion of the Product
- Product and Packaging design

Problem Solving: This type of key activity relates to creating new solutions to individual customer problems. Consumers/ customers have varying problems and a business modeled after problem solving usually aims to find unique solutions to these problems. Businesses like consultancy, hospitals, and every service organization have problem solving dominating their activities. Consequently, these businesses have activities focusing on knowledge management and continuous training as basics. For example, my tax consultancy firm ProTax Refunds is a problem-solving business and the value propositions include:

- Filing taxes for customers.
- Teaching customers how to file taxes.
- Saving customers the hassle and time involved in filing taxes.
- Helping customers get accurate tax refunds.
- Solving tax problems for customers.
- Promoting these services to customers through various marketing schemes in an educative manner.
- Performing other tax related functions.

By providing these services, we have learned and acquired information on repeat customers, and have gained knowledge to improve.

Platform/Network: This type of key activity is mostly carried out by businesses with models designed with a platform as key resource. They are dominated by platform or network related key activities. Networks, matchmaking platforms, software, and even brands can function as a platform. eBay's business model dictates that the company continually develops and maintain its platform: the website at eBay.com. Similarly, Visa's business model requires activities related to its Visa® credit card transaction platform for merchants, customers, and banks. Key activities in this category relate to platform management, service provisioning, and platform promotion.

COMMUNICATION/MARKETING

This is simply the way you communicate and market your value proposition to your prospective customers/consumers. There are different channels and tools used in combination to form an effective value proposition in business. The right Communication/Marketing or Marketing communication channels enables you to focus your product/service to its desired market or the general market. A Marketing Commutations tool can be anything from advertising, personal selling, direct marketing, sponsorship, communication and promotion, to public relations. So, a marketing communications strategy is the strategy used by your business to reach the target market through various types of communication. It includes your message (what is to be said), the medium (where it is said), and the target (to whom the message is intended). It includes advertising, promotions, sales, branding, and online promotions. This process allows the public to understand your brand and successful branding involves targeting audiences that appreciate your marketing program.

The process of starting my tax consultancy business, ProTax Refunds, provides a perfect illustration. One of my key activities when we started was to find out what our competition was doing and how they were doing it.

I realized that a lot of our competitors were using phone calls to reach customers, so we analyzed this and sought how we could apply this method. We then came up with customized text messages. These messages are short and concise, as well as direct and to the point. This method doesn't disturb customers' schedules. Our customers do not have to worry about taking phone calls when they are busy and can always go back to the text messages at their convenience. We looked at other complaints customers may have had with our competitors, and looked for ways to better them in serving the customers. Some of what we did include "Tax by Text," which was revolutionary. We took an educative tax approach by educating our clients with text messages that focused on the knowledge and not the irrelevances.

Our communication and marketing were designed to approach the customers in a different way from what our competitors were doing. Your goal should be to find out what the competition is doing, what complaints do customers have, and what you can do to improve it. Your communications and marketing strategy should be derived from that angle. At ProTax Refunds, we thought of how we could improve the tax experience for the customer by creating a unique experience from what our competitors offered. We approached our customers in a soft sell manner, and in an educational manner while pushing for a win-win situation between the business and the customers. We added value (knowledge) by educating them on different filing styles that exist, such as filing separatist, single, and etc. Also, we introduced workshops and seminars and created videos they could watch at their own time. In return, the customers gave us loyalty and support because we solved their problem in a different way, and educated them in the process.

Your communications and marketing tools should be used to deliver a clear and consistent message to your target audiences. It is traditionally known in business as the promotional element of the four PS in Marketing: Product, Place, Price, and Promotion. The primary goal is to reach your defined audience and effect behavior by informing, persuading, and reminding. Marketing communications helps your business to acquire new customers by building awareness and encouraging trial. This process also helps your business to maintain your current customer base by reinforcing their purchase behavior, by providing additional information about your brand's benefits. Your marketing plan identifies the key opportunities, threats, weaknesses and strengths, as well as sets objectives with an action plan to achieve the marketing goals. Each section of the 4Ps sets its own objective. For example, a Pricing objective might be to increase sales in a certain geographical area. Pricing is one of the most significant aspects of marketing that can change the whole market negatively or positively.

The Marketing Communications plan for my hair salon business was tailored similar to the Tax business. When we entered the market, we surveyed and researched into what our competitors had been doing, what customers liked, and what they had the most complaints about. We even called and shopped them to find out their rates, their services, and what discounts they were giving. Based on our discoveries, we set our pricing to the rates in the market and even offered lower prices in order to win customers over. We also gave discounts that were now the best in the market, while using a social media approach. This also gave us an edge. Furthermore, we incorporated some unique services that our competitors were not providing, which proved to be a huge draw for customers. Whatever marketing communications campaign you explore, three things are important: Brand Alignment, Customer Alignment, and Budget Alignment.

- **Brand Alignment:** Your marketing channel should have the same brand perception as yours.
- **Customer Alignment**: Follow the oldest rule in marketing: "be where your customers already are". This means, pick channels where your customers are already active.
- **Budget Alignment**: This is simply choosing a marketing channel that fits your budget.

SALE STRATEGIES

Identify a sales strategy or sales strategies for your business. A sales strategy is simply the plan by a business or individual on how to go about selling products and services and increase profits. These strategies are typically developed by the business owner, along with sales, marketing, and advertising managers. It features the use of, "pitches" or key points to address when approaching a potential customer. Some pitches may be memorized and communicated verbatim, some might be in the form of newsletters or emails. Although sales strategies differ by industry, no matter what you sell you need to determine a target market. A business selling baby dolls would be targeting the wrong market if it is advertised in fashion magazines. Identifying the market is deeper than just the obvious. Factors such as location, age, gender, and spending habits of potential customers must also be established.

Every business determines how to go about selling and promoting products when developing a sales strategy. Will you contact customers by mail, phone, or by sending out mass marketing emails? You can use all of the above methods and more, including meeting potential clients face-to-face. It all depends on your knowledge of the market and this is what informs how you plan your sales strategy. Much of how you go about pushing out products and services is determined by how much you know the market you are operating in. The best sales strategies are built with the competition in mind. Understating what has worked for opposing businesses and integrating it into your own sales strategy is key. You can do this by either offering a similar product/service at a lower price or by marketing your product as the best of its kind.

Good organization is a major factor for success in any industry and sales is not entirely different. Sales strategies need to include details on the role of those making sales, management of accounts and territories, and commission/compensation. Sometimes, sales strategies can even outline incentives and bonuses for a successful sales record. Your sales plan sets out the sales targets and tactics for your business and identifies the steps needed to meet those targets. A sale plan will help you:

- Define a set of sales targets.
- Choose sales strategies that are sited to your target market.
- Identify sales tactics for your sales team.
- Activate, motivate, and focus your sales team.
- Budget and clarify steps to take to achieve your targets.
- Review your goals periodically and improve your approaches to sales.

MAINTENANCE

Maintenance is also a very important aspect of communications and marketing. It is mainly the process of maintaining the business relationship between your business and the customers. Repeat customers in business are worth their weight in gold. Do everything in your power to maintain a positive business relationship between you and your customers. Phone calls, text messages, post cards, mail, and emails are different ways to maintain business relationships.

Maintaining relationships is important for the continued success of our business with our customers. Through positive word-of-mouth, your customers will be the champions to bring in new clients and provide an overall boom to the business. Many business owners may find doing this difficult, but the process is actually simple if followed precisely. Here are some proven techniques to employ:

- Send greeting cards
- Keep lines of communication open

- Know the stages of customer loyalty
- Provide customer support
- Ask for customers' opinions
- Don't overlook current customers in your marketing
- Adapt your business plan/model

Advise and educate your customers at will of the different products you have. It fosters maintenance.

Philippians 4:6-7 New King James Version (NKJV)
6 Be anxious for nothing, but in everything by prayer and supplication, with thanksgiving, let your requests be made known to God; 7 and the peace of God, which surpasses all understanding, will guard your hearts and minds through Christ Jesus.

Prayer
Dear Lord, help me not to be anxious for nothing. Give me clear direction in all of my activities, so that I may be effective in all that I do. In Jesus Name. Amen.

CHAPTER NINE

Cost/Profit Structure

The Bible emphasizes the concept of cost just like the whole Christian journey comes with a cost. Cost is also rooted in the concept of discipleship, such as when you accept Jesus Christ as your Lord and savior; there is a cost to follow him. Luke 14:33 says, *"So therefore, no one of you can be my disciple who does not give up all his own possessions"*. Salvation is the price and giving up sin is the cost. Cost in business includes all the costs (fixed, variable, direct, and indirect) incurred in carrying out the operations of the business. The Bible stresses the importance of cost in salvation and likewise, you will need to learn that cost is one of the most important concepts in business. A business owner has to be able to determine the costs of the products or services they offer for sale. Before I start any business, I usually start with determining my costs and also the cost of a customer. There are different types of costs, such as direct and indirect costs, that an entrepreneur must understand to effectively run a business.

Cost determines profit and is very vital to making decisions, in both small and large businesses. There is a general tendency to confuse cost for price, but both business terms are markedly different. The amount your business charges customers per unit of the product or service it sells is price. The amount it takes for your company to produce the product or service it sells is the cost. The difference between price, the amount charged to the customer, and cost, the expense to produce the item, is the profit or net income. These terms are interwoven but very different. It is necessary to duly understand them. Cost defines all the expenses your business incurs in creating the products or services you offer for sale. Cost also helps you determine your profit or net income and that makes it pertinent for any business. There are different types of business costs:

- **Variable Cost**: The variable cost is the cost which changes with any change in production. This can be raw material, wages of labor, energy used in production, and others.

- **Fixed Cost**: Fixed cost is the cost which remains fixed irrespective of the level of output. Examples of fixed cost include rent, salaries of employees, advertising, and promotional campaigns.

- **Direct Cost**: The Direct Cost is the cost assigned to the production of certain goods and services, such as labor, material, fuel, power, or any other expense related to the production of a product is the direct cost.

- **Indirect Cost**: The Indirect Cost is the cost which cannot be directly attributed to the production of goods and services. Depreciation, supervision, security, maintenance, and administrative expenses are the cost incurred, which cannot be assigned to a specific product or department; hence, they are classified as Indirect Cost.

Business cost is computed to determine the efficiency of running your business operations. Many terms surround the word, "cost" in the business world. It refers to the product produced by a business for which a separate measure of cost is desired. It is also a little more complex than that because it can also refer to a service, a customer or a project and is used when allocating direct or indirect costs. For instance, when taking a course in college, that course is the cost object. The cost itself is that of tuition and books. The cost of the foregone alternative of working instead of going to school is the opportunity cost.

There are two main categories of cost structure: value driven and cost-driven. Value driven cost structure is focused on creating more value in the product itself, not necessarily producing at the lowest possible cost. Gucci, Hublot, Rolex, Bentley, and Ritz-Carlton are prototypes of value driven cost structure. Cost-driven structure focuses on minimizing the costs of the product or service as much as possible. Walmart would fall under this category. You must consider the most important costs to your business operations and create a hypothesis for these expenses. Taking into account both fixed costs, such as startup and acquisition costs and variable costs, or your monthly operating costs, is highly important. To succeed in business, your costs will have to be less than your revenue. If that is not the case, then a lot of adjustments will need to be made.

Deciding to start a business is an exciting moment for any new entrepreneur, but that excitement is often accompanied by anxiety and uncertainty. Many of these anxieties and doubts stem from financial worries, worrying about whether the business will be profitable in the long term, as well as the startup costs. Some entrepreneurs have made the gross mistake of jumping into a business without thinking carefully enough about business costs, and whether or not the costs are feasible. There is more to business than furnishings, office space, and a website. In the preliminary stage of starting a business, start-up costs require careful planning and meticulous accounting. A few entrepreneurs neglect this process, relying instead on a flood of customers to keep the business afloat. This usually brings abysmal business results. Creating your business plan entails estimating your startup cost and planning ahead to position yourself for success. Underestimating expenses is a situation that does not bode well for any business owner.

You must employ a meticulous approach to determine the exact cost of running your business. Just like the cost of accepting and following Christ is very emphasized by God, a business owner ought to determine cost before delving into any business. For all the businesses I have ventured in, this has been a guiding principle for me. I set out to determine my costs before even starting the business.

I look at my monthly expenses, build a budget for it and on my budget, I put all my fixed and variable costs. This will help me figure out how much my business will need to make every month to cover overhead. Assuming my start up is $10,000, then my business would need to make about $825 a month for me to recoup my investment in one year. I put in a fixed expense to reimburse my initial investment. I also set out periodic targets of when I want to break even; this can be 12 months or 24 months, depending on the type of business. After that, I add up all fixed expenses, such as rent and variable cost and this helps me determine what the cost to run the particular business might be.

Startup costs are the expenses incurred during the process of creating your new business. There are various types of businesses and they all require different types of startup costs. Online businesses require different startup costs than brick-and-mortars, just like a restaurant requires different startup costs than a hair salon. However, the following expenses are common to all business types:

Advertising & Promotion: A new business requires promotion to succeed, and includes everything a company does in order to attract clients to the business from local ads, handbills, to even social media posts.

Borrowing Costs: Starting up a business requires an infusion of capital and there are two ways to acquire capital for a business: equity financing and debt financing. Equity financing entails the issuance of stocks and usually applies to large scale businesses. Small businesses source financing from debt that comes in a form of a small business loan. Loans can be from banks or saving institutions and accompanied by interest payment. These payments must be planned for when starting a business, as the cost of default is brutal.

Employee Expenses: If you are starting a business, you must plan for wages, salaries, and benefits (also known as the cost of labor). Inadequate compensation for employee would result in low morale, mutiny, and bad publicity.

Equipment and Supplies: Every business requires some form of equipment and basic supplies. Before adding equipment expenses to the startup cost, a decision has to be made to lease or buy. This decision depends absolutely on your budget.

Insurance, License, and Permit Fees: Many businesses are expected to submit health inspections, and authorizations, as well as obtain certain business licenses and permits. Some businesses might require basic licenses, while others need industry-specific permits. Carrying insurance to cover your employees, customers, business, and yourself can help protect your personal assets from any liabilities that may arise.

Research Expenses: Careful research of the industry and the customer segment must be conducted before starting a business venture. Some business owners choose to hire research firms and others choose to do it by themselves. The expenses incurred is listed under research expenses and should be added to the start up cost.

Technological Expenses: These expenses include the cost of a website, information systems, and software for a business.

It is always advisable to have some extra money set aside for any overlooked or unexpected expenses. Most businesses fail due to lack of cash to deal with unexpected problems during the business season. The start-up costs for a sole proprietorship business will differ from a business with a partnership or corporation. Some additional costs that will be incurred by a partnership include the legal cost of drafting a partnership agreement and state registration fees. Other costs that will be incurred by a corporation include fees for filing articles of incorporation, bylaws, and terms of original stock certificates. Launching a new business can be invigorating, but getting caught up in the excitement and neglecting details would lead to failure.

PRODUCT OR MANUFACTURING COSTS

The only relevant costs in product costing are the costs in the production department. This consists of direct and indirect costs of producing a product in a manufacturing firm. Products are inventories, and costs are recorded in an inventory account until the units are sold. Then the costs to produce those units get transferred to the cost of goods sold account. Product costs consists of direct materials, direct labor, and manufacturing overhead. The total product cost is the sum of the three. Indirect materials and indirect labor are usually included in overhead. Let's use the following example to calculate the total product cost and total per unit cost:

Troy Corporation produces widgets at the rate 30,000 units per week. Last week, their direct materials were $50,000, direct labor was $40,000, and overhead was $80,000. With the information above, we can calculate the total product cost and cost per unit:

Direct Materials: $50,000
Direct Lab: $40,000
Overhead: $80,000
Total Product Cost: $170,000

Per Unit cost would be $170,000/30,000 units = $5.67 per widget.

Product costs generally fall under two categories: prime costs and conversion costs. Prime costs include direct materials plus direct labor, while conversion costs include direct labor cost and manufacturing overhead cost. Conversion costs are simply the costs of converting raw materials into the final product.

All other costs of running the business aside the product costs are called period costs. Super Bowl ads, for example, are period costs. Other examples include salaries and wages, as well as the costs of office supplies. Period costs do not appear as inventory on the balance sheet, it appears as expenses on income statement. If a period cost is expected to generate an economic benefit beyond one year, then it can be capitalized, or recorded as an asset on the company's balance sheet, and written off as depreciation over a few years.

PROFIT STRUCTURE

Profit is very essential in business and anybody going into business hopes to make profit, otherwise it is not worth the while. The Bible says in Proverbs 14:23: *"In all toil there is profit, but mere talk tends only to poverty."* The concept of profit is further emphasized in Mark 8:36: *"For what shall it profit a man if he shall gain the whole world, and lose his soul."* Profit in business is the financial benefit that is realized when the amount of revenue gained from a business activity exceeds the expenses, costs, and taxes needed to sustain the business activity. Regardless of if a business is just a couple of kids running a lemonade stand or multinational company, consistently earning profit is every business owner's goal. Therefore, much of business performance is based on profitability in its various forms. Some analysts are interested in top-line profitability, whereas others are interested in profitability before expenses, such as taxes and interest. Some are only concerned with profitability after all expenses have been paid.

There are three major types of profit that come into reckoning in the business world: Gross Profit, Operating Profit, and Net Profit. Each type gives more information about any business performance, especially when compared against other time periods and industry competitors. All three levels of profitability are recorded on the income statement.

Gross Profit: This is the first level of profitability. Gross profit is sales minus the cost of goods sold. Sales is the first item you have on the income statement, and the costs of goods sold (COGS) is generally listed below it. For example, if my business has $100,000 in sales and a COGS of $60,000, it means my gross profit is $40,000 or $100,000 minus $60,000. Divide gross profit by sales for the gross profit margin, which turns out to be 40% or $40,000 divided by $100,000.

Operating Profit: This is the second level of profitability in business. Operating profit is calculated by deducting operating expenses from gross profit. Gross profit looks at profitability after direct expenses and operating profit looks at profitability after operating expenses. These are things like selling, general and administrative costs (SG&A). If your company has $20,000 in operating expenses, the operating profit is $40,000 minus $20,000, equaling $20,000. Divide operating profit by sales for the operating profit margin, which is 20%.

Net Profit: Net Profit is the third level of profitability in business. It is the income left over after all expenses, including taxes, and interest have been paid. If interest is $5,000 and taxes are another $5,000, net profit is calculated by deducting both of these from operating profit. In the example of the business used above, the answer is $20,000 minus $10,000, which equals $10,000. Divide net profit by sales for the net profit margin.

Luke 14:28

[28] *"For which of you, intending to build a tower, does not sit down first and count the cost, whether he has enough to finish it."*

Prayer

Lord, you said in your Word to count the cost, Lord, reveal every resource that is needed to complete each project or assignment. I believe that provision belongs to you. So please bless me with the right relationships and strategy needed in order to receive what you have for me to complete what I set out to do. Amen!

References

Brian, Tracy. (2005). *Choosing a Product or Service to Sell*. Retrieved from https://www.entrepreneur.com/article78778

Elaine, J. Hom. (2013). *What is B2C?*
Retrieved from https://www.businessnewsdaily.com

Will, Kenton. (2019). *Business-to-Consumer* (B2C).
Retrieved from https://www.investopedia.com/terms/b/btoc.asp

Will, Kenton. (2019). *What is Distribution Channel?*
Retrieved from https://www.investopedia.com/terms/d/distribution-channel.asp

C.Uzialko. (2019). *What is B2b?*
Retrieved from https://www.businessnewsdaily.com/500-what-is-b2b.html

Bernazzani, Sophia. Originally published Nov 13, 2018, updated March 12 2019. *14 Examples of Customer Retention Strategies that Work*. Retrieved from https://blog.hubspot.com/service/customer-retention-strategies

Joanne. (2017). *So You want to Start a Membership Business*. Retrieved from https://memberhouse.com/membership/so-you- want-to-start-amembership-business/. Retrieved from WHYISCUSTOMERSERVICEIMPORTANT

(AUGUST 2016)? https://www.performanceinpeople.co.uk/ blog/why-is-customer-service-important/\

Revenue Streams. Retrieved from https://www.inc.com/ encyclopedia/revenue-streams.html

Key Resources. Retrieved from http://www.ecommerce-digest.com/key-resources.html

Anastasia. (2015). *Key Resources Building Block in Business Model Canvas*. Retrieved fromhttps://www.cleverism. com/ke y-resources-building-block-in-business-model-canvas/

Anastasia. (2015). *Key Partners in Business Model Canvas Key Partnerships*. Retrieved from https://www.cleverism.com/key-partners-in-business- model-canvas/

Anastasia. (2015). *Key Activities Block in Business. Model Canvas*. Retrieved from https://www.cleverism.com/key-activities-block-busines s-model-canvas/

Dragilev, Dmitry. (2019). *Marketing Communications Strategy: What It is & How to Do It Right*. Retrieved from https://www.criminallyprolific.com/marketing-communications-strategy/

Amico, Sam. *Definition of Sales Strategy*. Retrieved from https://smallbusiness.chron.com/definition-sales-strategy-2213. html

COST STRUCTURE. RETRIEVED FROM

http://www.ecommerce-digest.com/cost-structure.html

https://corporatefinanceinstitute.com/resources/knowledge/finance/cost-structure/

http://www.ecommerce-digest.com/key-partnerships.

html https:/www.Investopedia.com https://wwww.

businessnewsdaily.com https://www.tutor2u.net

https://www.insightly.com https://www.wikipedia.com https://www.hustletostartup.com https://www.business.com

CHAPTER ONE NOTES

_____

_____

_____

_____

_____

_____

_____

_____

_____

_____

_____

_____

_____

_____

_____

_____

_____

_____

_____

_____

CHAPTER ONE NOTES

CHAPTER TWO NOTES

_____

_____

_____

_____

_____

_____

_____

_____

_____

_____

_____

_____

_____

_____

_____

_____

_____

_____

_____

_____

_____

_____

_____

_____

CHAPTER TWO NOTES

CHAPTER THREE NOTES

_____

_____

_____

_____

_____

_____

_____

_____

_____

_____

_____

_____

_____

_____

_____

_____

_____

_____

_____

_____

_____

_____

_____

CHAPTER THREE NOTES

_____

_____

_____

_____

_____

_____

_____

_____

_____

_____

_____

_____

_____

_____

_____

_____

_____

_____

_____

_____

_____

_____

CHAPTER FOUR NOTES

CHAPTER FOUR NOTES

CHAPTER FIVE NOTES

CHAPTER FIVE NOTES

CHAPTER SIX NOTES

CHAPTER SIX NOTES

CHAPTER SEVEN NOTES

_____

_____

_____

_____

_____

_____

_____

_____

_____

_____

_____

_____

_____

_____

_____

_____

_____

_____

_____

_____

_____

_____

_____

_____

CHAPTER SEVEN NOTES

_____

_____

_____

_____

_____

_____

_____

_____

_____

_____

_____

_____

_____

_____

_____

_____

_____

_____

_____

_____

_____

_____

_____

_____

_____

_____

CHAPTER EIGHT NOTES

_____

_____

_____

_____

_____

_____

_____

_____

_____

_____

_____

_____

_____

_____

_____

_____

_____

_____

_____

_____

_____

_____

CHAPTER EIGHT NOTES

CHAPTER NINE NOTES

CHAPTER NINE NOTES

_____

_____

_____

_____

_____

_____

_____

_____

_____

_____

_____

_____

_____

_____

_____

_____

_____

_____

_____

_____

_____

About the Author

Rudy Mutombo is a serial entrepreneur who believes in coaching individuals into success. Being a Congolese-American, he's been able to have a great advantage by bridging the international gap that stands between great global partnerships. His ability to help people maximize their potential has made him a well sought-after coach and advisor. Rudy Mutombo values intact work ethics, and he is a great example of perseverance. His business academy is the breeding ground for international success.

FOR COACHING SESSION CONTACT:

1825 Walnut Hill Ln., Ste. 120
Irving, Texas 75038

Phone Number: 866-231-8251
Fax: 214-614-8436

Email Address: info@rudymutombo.com

.